T0330122

REGULATING HUMAN RESEARCH

REGULATING HUMAN RESEARCH

IRBs from Peer Review to Compliance Bureaucracy

SARAH BABB

STANFORD UNIVERSITY PRESS

Stanford, California

STANFORD UNIVERSITY PRESS
Stanford, California

© 2020 by the Board of Trustees of the Leland Stanford Junior University.
All rights reserved.

No part of this book may be reproduced or transmitted in any form or by any means, electronic or mechanical, including photocopying and recording, or in any information storage or retrieval system without the prior written permission of Stanford University Press.

Printed in the United States of America on acid-free, archival-quality paper

LIBRARY OF CONGRESS CATALOGING-IN-PUBLICATION DATA

Names: Babb, Sarah L., author.
Title: Regulating human research : IRBs from peer review to compliance
    bureaucracy / Sarah Babb.
Description: Stanford, California : Stanford University Press, 2020. |
    Includes bibliographical references and index.
Identifiers: LCCN 2019019676 (print) | LCCN 2019021745 (ebook) |
    ISBN 9781503611238 (electronic) | ISBN 9781503610149 (cloth : alk. paper) |
    ISBN 9781503611221 (pbk. : alk. paper)
Subjects: LCSH: Institutional review boards (Medicine)—United States. |
    Human experimentation in medicine—Law and legislation—United States. |
    Medical ethics committees—United States. | Bureaucracy—United States.
Classification: LCC R852.5 (ebook) | LCC R852.5 .B33 2020 (print) |
    DDC 174.2/8—dc23
LC record available at https://lccn.loc.gov/2019019676

Cover design: Christian Fuenfhausen

Typeset by Westchester Publishing Services in 10/14 Minion Pro

To my father, Alan Babb, who got me thinking about this topic, who gave me a title, and whose insight and encouragement helped me get to this book.

Contents

Acknowledgments

I am deeply grateful to all the informants who took the time to share their professional world with me. Many thanks to Julia Hughes for her expert excavation of congressional documents, to Liz Brennan for helping me get started, to Steven Bao for his timely formatting assistance, to Larissa Truchan for her careful proofreading, and to Janice Irvine and Leslie Salzinger for their ongoing faith in the importance of this topic. Thanks also to Public Responsibility in Medicine and Research for granting me access to their membership statistics. My research was supported by a series of research expense grants from Boston College.

I extend special thanks to the people who took time to read over drafts of sections of this book, offered suggestions, and corrected misunderstandings: Michel Anteby, Rebecca Armstrong, Lois Brako, Lisa Crossley, Leonard Glantz, Alya Guseva, Erica Heath, Adam Hedgecoe, Eric Mah, Shep Melnick, Smitha Radhakrishnan, Susan Rose, and Suzanne Rivera. A particularly heartfelt thanks to Tom Puglisi, who not only shared with me his extensive experiences as a regulator, but also very patiently walked me through how the regulations work. Any remaining mistakes and misinterpretations are, of course, my own.

REGULATING HUMAN RESEARCH

Introduction

"ALL I KNEW was that they just kept saying I had the bad blood—they never mentioned syphilis to me. Not even once," recalled Charles Pollard, one of the last survivors of the infamous Tuskegee syphilis study. Like the other men in the decades-long study, Charles had been cruelly misinformed. Researchers told the men—all African American, and mostly poor and illiterate—that they were being treated for "bad blood." In fact, they had unknowingly signed up for a study of the effects of untreated syphilis. When penicillin was found to be an effective cure, they were neither offered the drug nor told that they had the disease; some were even prevented from being treated. Instead, they were monitored for decades; when they died, their bodies were examined postmortem. The study had received millions of dollars in federal funding.[1]

It was public outrage over Tuskegee and other similarly horrifying abuses that led the U.S. Congress to pass the National Research Act in 1974. The act created an expert commission that would produce the Belmont Report, which laid out principles for the ethical treatment of human subjects. The report established that although biomedical studies could lead to lifesaving discoveries, they could not be allowed to violate the human rights of the people who participate in them. Studies should minimize the risk of harm to participants and strike a balance between risk and potential benefits. They should strive to ensure that subjects participate voluntarily, with a full understanding of the nature of the research, and only after being selected in a fair, nonexploitative manner. The Belmont principles remain the bedrock of human research ethics in the United States today.

Ethics are moral principles that guide behavior. Sometimes they provide clear answers about what we should and should not do—for example, there is no conceivable reading of the Belmont principles that could justify the Tuskegee study. In other cases, ethics provide parameters for thoughtful debates in which reasonable people can disagree. Should we allow a study in which there is a small risk of serious physical harm, but also a strong likelihood of life-saving benefits? Should we be more worried about a small risk of serious harm or a large risk of a minor harm? These are among the many complex questions that must be considered when weighing the ethics of studies on human beings.

In contrast, regulations are government rules that require certain actions while prohibiting others. The same National Research Act that chartered the Belmont Report also authorized federal regulations. Their purpose was to provide a legal framework to protect human research subjects from ethical abuses. The principal requirement of these regulations was that federally funded research with human subjects be reviewed by committees known as Institutional Review Boards (IRBs).

Today, IRBs are best known for making ethical decisions based on the Belmont principles—for weighing research proposals to determine whether risks to human subjects are reasonable, and whether subjects are being provided with adequate opportunity to give their informed consent. Yet, in addition to making ethical judgments, IRBs are also charged with the less glamorous role of managing compliance with federal regulations.

This regulatory dimension first came to my attention back in 2009, when I began a three-year term on the Boston College IRB. As a faculty board member, I was charged with applying not only the Belmont ethics, but also a more perplexing set of guidelines. For example, there was a list of eight standard elements of informed consent, required by the regulations except when the researcher obtained either a waiver of one or more elements of informed consent or a waiver of documentation of informed consent. Each kind of waiver had a different list of similarly bewildering eligibility criteria.

I remember feeling anxious the first time I was exposed to these regulatory minutiae—and hoping that there were others better qualified than I to remember and apply them.

As it turned out, I was not expected to master these important but confusing technicalities. Instead, my board colleagues and I regularly relied on IRB staff for guidance on regulatory matters. Over time, I came to understand that the image of IRBs as committees charged with weighing ethical dilemmas captured the tip of a much larger iceberg of activities. I could see that there was a more routine form of regulatory decision making that was important, but not widely understood or even acknowledged. My desire to understand it led me to the research that culminated in this book.

From Amateur Board to Compliance Bureaucracy

For historical reasons, IRBs resemble peer review committees. Most are located at research institutions, such as universities and academic medical centers, and are mostly composed of faculty volunteers who make ethical judgments based on their scholarly expertise.

Much of what has been written about these boards has focused on these panels of scholars making careful ethical decisions.[2] What is frequently overlooked is that most IRB decisions today are not made by convened committees of academics at all. For example, the decision to approve the research for this book was made not by a faculty volunteer but by staff members in the IRB office, who reviewed my application for exemption. My informed consent form and verbal script were based on staff-designed templates. Had my research involved higher levels of risk, it would eventually have been discussed by faculty board members, but only after being revised in consultation with staff.

In fact, until about twenty years ago, IRBs could accurately be described as the faculty-run committees that remain in the popular imaginary today. They were typically managed by faculty chairpersons—usually uncompensated—with the assistance of a single clerical staff member. "The [faculty] chairman [*sic*] is probably the most important member on the IRB," explained two Tufts biomedical researchers at a conference in 1980. "It is incumbent upon the chairman to be fully informed about the current status of the regulations and in turn educate the members of the IRB."[3]

Sometime around the late 1990s, however, IRBs began their metamorphosis into something different. Precipitating the change was a new round of research scandals, which triggered a wave of federal enforcement actions. Regulators began to scrutinize IRB operations more closely, and disciplined a number of prominent research institutions. In response to this risky environment, these institutions began to invest in IRB administration. The trend was muted at liberal arts colleges, where there was little sponsored research to penalize. However, investment in IRB offices was quite rapid and pronounced at federally funded research universities and medical centers—and most especially at institutions with large amounts of federally sponsored biomedical research.

At these organizations, there was a startling increase in the number of staff: by 2007, more than half of respondents in a survey of the IRB world reported that their offices had three or more full-time staff members, with some reporting offices three times that size or more.[4] Meanwhile, there was a significant upgrading in qualifications of staff members, an increasing proportion of whom had advanced postgraduate degrees. These were no longer secretaries working under the supervision of IRB faculty chairs, but rather research administrators, embedded in a chain of command reaching up to the highest level of administration, and with a growing sense of professional identity.

Where this transformation occurred, there was a rearrangement of decision making, as illustrated in figure I.1. In the old model, the main job of staff was to manage the paperwork; decisions were made by faculty volunteers. In the emerging new model, staff took charge of many important decisions, such as whether research qualified for exemption, or how investigators should modify their submission before bringing it to the board. More experienced and qualified staff became board members who could vote on the riskiest studies and also approve expedited protocols. Faculty volunteers continued to make up a majority on boards and to consider weighty ethical decisions. However, at most research institutions, decisions that required regulatory knowledge were turned over to staff.

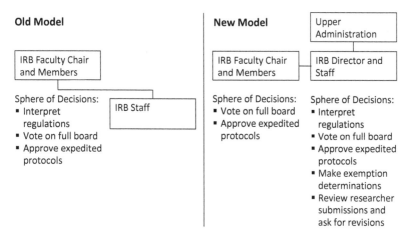

FIGURE I.1. Two models of IRB decision making.

In this way, volunteer committees gave way to compliance bureaucracy. I do not use the term "bureaucracy" in the colloquial sense, with its inherently negative connotations of red tape and ineptitude. Rather, I wish to invoke the term as it was used by the German sociologist Max Weber, who thought that bureaucracy was a uniquely effective way of organizing work on a large scale. A bureaucratic system was based on written rules and records as well as a clear division of labor. The people who labored in bureaucracies were professionals—they were hired and promoted based on their expert qualifications and performance, and were paid a salary.

For Weber, bureaucracy was key to the flourishing of modern social life. It was particularly important to the rise of the modern nation-state. Aided by powerful bureaucratic machinery, states could develop modern militaries, taxation systems, social security administrations, and systems of regulation.

Yet IRBs are not government offices. With few exceptions, the people in charge of overseeing compliance with the regulations are not federal employees.[5] In this book, I define a *compliance bureaucracy* as a nongovernmental office that uses skilled staff—compliance professionals—to interpret, apply, and oversee adherence to government rules. This book tells the story of how

IRBs evolved from volunteer committees into compliance bureaucracies, and what some of the consequences have been.

Compliance Bureaucracy as Workaround

I was in the lobby of a sleek glass office building in Rockville, Maryland, trying to get my bearings. As I peered at the directory, I could see that there were many tenants. There were two wealth management firms, a company that specialized in human resources consulting, a health care technology company, and a medical office specializing in neurological diseases of the ear. There were also several satellite offices of the U.S. Department of Health and Human Services. One was the Office for Human Research Protections (OHRP), which occupied a single suite on the second floor—more than enough space for its twenty-two employees.

This small, unassuming office is responsible for overseeing more than ten thousand IRBs at research institutions across the United States, and in many other countries as well. Because the size of the office's staff is miniscule in proportion to this jurisdiction, the office usually conducts an audit only when it learns of a problem. It lacks the authority to issue formal precedents, although it can issue "guidance," as long as it does not stray too far from the original regulatory meaning.

In spite of OHRP's apparent weakness, in some ways it is quite powerful. Hanging on its every word are many thousands of locally financed IRB offices, each with its own staff, policies, and procedures. OHRP occupies the apex of a regulatory pyramid, atop an enormous base of compliance bureaucracies. Sharing this top position are departments within the Food and Drug Administration charged with enforcing a separate set of IRB regulations. It is common for IRBs to follow both sets of rules.

This system exemplifies the quirkiness of American governance, which occurs through "an immensely complex tangle of indirect incentives, cross-cutting regulations, overlapping jurisdictions, delegated responsibility, and diffuse accountability."[6] Scholars have coined various terms that refer to different aspects of this phenomenon, including "delegated governance," the "litigation state," the "associational state," and the "Rube Goldberg state."[7]

For lack of a more comprehensive alternative, I have chosen the term "workaround state" to describe the dynamics I describe in this book. Its defining characteristic is the outsourcing of functions that in other industrial democracies are seen as the purview of central government. The American health care system delegates much of the job of insuring citizens to private firms and fifty state governments.[8] Private companies are tasked with stabilizing the residential mortgage market; and, in the absence of a robust technocratic civil service, policy ideas are supplied by private think tanks.[9] We have even embraced private prisons in our penal system.[10]

These and innumerable other examples of delegation can be seen as workarounds—alternative means to ends that the federal government cannot or will not pursue. They emerge because attempts to use federal power to pursue important policy goals are often thwarted by characteristically American policy obstacles, including underdeveloped administrative capacity, federalism, divided government, and antigovernment political ideology. These make it difficult for policy makers to overcome the opposition of organized interest groups, and lead to the emergence of workarounds.[11] Sometimes workarounds represent a deliberate strategy for expanding state capacity while avoiding the political controversy and expense of big government.[12] In other cases, they emerge organically to fill in the gaps left by the absence of government activity.[13]

One variety of workaround is compliance bureaucracy. Although the term "compliance bureaucracy" is my own, the phenomenon it represents is well known among organizational sociologists. Over the past several decades, American organizations have spun off a variety of subunits dedicated to managing compliance in diverse areas, such as health care privacy, financial services, and employment law.[14] A key role of these offices is to make sense of government rules. In the United States, political and institutional limitations on state-building result in fragile and fragmented regulatory authority. Organizations receive weak, inconsistent, and confusing signals about what it means to comply. To adapt to this risky environment, they create specialized offices staffed by skilled workers.[15]

Significantly, compliance professionals do much more than merely advise organizations on how to follow government rules. They design, implement, and manage their own local systems of oversight, and enforcement, known as "compliance programs"; they also clarify the meaning of statutes and regulations by developing professional norms or "best practices"—standards that can spread nationwide, and even be endorsed by the government.[16] In the United States, compliance bureaucracy is a powerful regulatory force in its own right. In other countries, where more capable state agencies exercise stronger oversight and send clearer signals, compliance bureaucracy is underdeveloped or absent; the staff members managing compliance are both fewer and less skilled, since their job is simply to follow the government's instructions.[17]

The protection of human research subjects is a critically important area of government oversight, and is recognized as such by industrialized democracies around the world. All require human research proposals to be evaluated by special committees.[18] These national systems delegate judgment to committees because ethics review is unamenable to micromanagement and blanket prohibitions: it must allow for thoughtful debates about intractable dilemmas in particular cases, and these must include the voices of experts who understand the research being proposed.

These fundamental similarities aside, what sets the American system apart is its extraordinary *degree* of delegation.[19] In many wealthy democracies, research ethics committees are more directly managed by national governments. In both France and the United Kingdom, for example, a researcher initiating a clinical trial typically goes through a national application system and is assigned to a government-coordinated committee. Government offices emit and regularly revise extensive standards for how these bodies carry out their duties.[20] By contrast, our American IRB system is more profoundly decentralized. Here, there are thousands of local boards, each with jurisdiction over its own local investigators, each developing its own policies and procedures, and all answerable to agencies that cannot engage in close monitoring, precedent-setting, or even regular policy updates. This provides fertile ground for the flourishing of compliance bureaucracy.

IRBs as a Special Case

Whether they deal with employment, privacy, or human research protections, compliance bureaucracies share a common vocation: the definition and application of federal rules. Yet IRBs are also unusual among compliance bureaucracies because for much of their history they were amateur-run, collegial bodies. In contrast, most other areas of compliance—such as privacy, financial services, and equal opportunity—were always the domain of paid staff.

Because IRBs had to *become* compliance bureaucracies, their history provides a unique perspective on what these bureaucracies do. Organizational sociologists have often emphasized the symbolic function of compliance bureaucracy, based on the example of civil rights law and equal opportunity (EEO) administration. The EEO case suggests that compliance offices exist not only to make sense of federal rules, but also to create "a visible commitment to law" to serve as "window dressing," and to show that organizations are "doing [their] best to figure out how to comply."[21]

Yet in the case of IRBs, this account leaves some important questions unanswered. For decades, faculty-run boards served as symbols of ethical and regulatory rectitude. The subsequent shift away from volunteer committees had a very high price tag: a 2007 survey found that the median annual cost of running an IRB at an academic medical center was $781,224, with staff salaries accounting for the biggest portion of the expense.[22] Over time, a growing number of biomedical studies were outsourced to for-profit "independent IRBs," which charged substantial fees. For example, in 2018 the largest of these for-profit boards charged $1,864 per study, with a surcharge of $1,076 per principal investigator, and additional fees levied for continuing review, extra consent documents, and protocol changes.[23]

What are organizations paying for when they invest in IRB offices or when they outsource compliance work to for-profit boards? I contend that to answer this question, we need to take seriously the classical Weberian view of bureaucracy's "purely technical superiority" over other forms of organizing work.[24] This technical role has not been emphasized in literature on compliance offices, most of which is based on equal opportunity and compliance with civil rights law.

The focus on EEO has left important variations across compliance fields unexplored. EEO offices occupy a field in which the boundaries of compliance are largely defined by courts in lawsuits, and where federal rules require relatively few tangible outputs.[25] The mechanism underlying compliance is the private right of action embedded in the Civil Rights Act of 1964, which allows individuals and public interest groups to sue for damages and to recoup legal costs if they win. If organizations want clarification on the meaning of compliance, they can look to the outcomes of legal battles as a guide.[26]

However, the National Research Act—the statute authorizing the IRB regulations—does not contain a private right of action, and IRB-related lawsuits are rare.[27] Instead, compliance is assessed in audits—formal investigations conducted by federal regulators.[28] Because auditing agencies are not empowered to set ethical precedents, they mainly assess whether IRBs have been upholding the administrative procedures that the regulations require— whether decisions are made by duly constituted committees, having considered the mandated criteria, having followed local policies, and so on.[29] In an audit, an IRB office will need to provide evidence that all the requisite procedures were followed each and every time a decision was made. To this end, they must provide auditors with voluminous, meticulously recorded documentation. Federal agencies may be understaffed, and the possibility of an audit remote; yet in the unlikely event of such an audit, failure to produce the proper documentation could get an organization in serious trouble.[30]

The central role of the audit in IRB compliance creates two sorts of technical problem—each better addressed by bureaucracy than by the labor of volunteers. The first is ensuring that complex procedural rules get followed to the letter and scrupulously documented. Faculty volunteers are not very good at attending to such minutiae. Even if we are interested in the regulations, we usually lack the time to master them, to oversee their routine implementation, and to create a scrupulous paper trail.

In contrast, bureaucracy is ideally suited to the painstaking work of mass-producing auditable compliance. As Weber observed long ago, bureaucracy demands "the full working capacity" of its officials, who "by constant practice [increase] their expertise."[31] Paid, full-time administrators can give their undivided attention to the technical features of the rules, and thereby ensure the satisfaction of auditing regulators. Such attention to detail is particularly important where different government agencies have overlapping but not entirely consistent requirements, creating additional layers of complexity that demand workers' dedicated concentration.

The second technical problem addressed by bureaucracy is the high cost of compliance. Following complex procedural rules and mass-producing auditable documents can interfere significantly with valued activities and can generate large financial expenses. Bureaucracy, although not popularly known for its cost-saving qualities, can be quite effective at controlling, standardizing, and routinizing human behavior to make processes faster and less time-consuming. These advantages make bureaucracy an invaluable tool for controlling the cost of compliance.

In this book, I argue that human research protection bureaucracies supplanted amateur IRBs both because they could make sense of the rules and because they were better equipped to manage the demands of auditable compliance. They could meet regulators' demand for precisely recorded, auditable indicators, while addressing organizations' need for efficiency, as compliance became increasingly intrusive and expensive. This evolution from amateur board to compliance bureaucracy had many consequences, both intended and unintended, which I describe in the chapters that follow.

Plan of the Book

The book is based on a wide variety of sources, including interviews with more than fifty individuals in and around the IRB world. Most were either current or former IRB administrators working on the front lines of regulatory compliance; others included former regulators, consultants, and faculty IRB members. My informants are described in greater detail in the appendix.

In chapter 1, I trace the origins and demise of a period I call the "era of approximate compliance," which lasted until roughly the late 1990s. During this time, IRBs were typically run by faculty volunteers who, while taking their ethical duties seriously, often paid little attention to the letter of the regulations. The regulatory system left ethical decisions to local boards and relied on the labor of unpaid faculty volunteers. It was overseen by federal offices with limited authority and resources. As the world of biomedical research became larger, more commercialized, and more complex, this framework became increasingly inadequate and out of date, creating the conditions for an outbreak of research scandals—and for a disciplinary crackdown on research institutions.

In chapter 2, I describe the circumstances that gave rise to the IRB profession, a new category of expert worker. By sanctioning institutions for noncompliance—while failing to fully define what it meant to comply—federal authorities created high levels of uncertainty. Research institutions responded in two ways. First, they adopted the most conservative reading of the regulations, thereby launching an "era of hypercompliance." Second, they hired skilled staff to interpret and apply these regulations, leading to the emergence of a nationwide human research protection profession.

In chapter 3, I show how IRB offices responded to powerful pressures to become more efficient. During the era of hypercompliance, the IRB review process came to pose an unacceptable obstruction to the biomedical research enterprise. In response, IRB offices deployed tools of bureaucratic administration to lower the cost of compliance. The rationalization of these offices definitively shifted the locus of decision making from faculty volunteers to full-time administrators and was the defining characteristic of the "era of compliance with efficiency," which began toward the middle of the first decade of the 2000s. This reorientation had unintended consequences, including frictions around the exercise of bureaucratic authority over research design, and goal displacement.

In chapter 4, I show how the IRB world came to adopt the dynamics, practices, and rhetoric of a private industry. This trend was uneven, and most visible in independent IRBs: boards run as for-profit enterprises, and mostly reviewing privately sponsored biomedical research. Yet standards set in the most industrialized sector spread throughout the human research protections world, fueled by the forces of market competition, private accreditation, and professionals' inclination to borrow widely accepted best practices.

In chapter 5, I analyze the expansion of IRB oversight to social and humanities research. With the federal crackdown, these researchers suddenly became enmeshed in a regulatory system designed around the routines of biomedical and other experimental studies. The shift was produced not by new rules, but by changed interpretations of these rules by local institutions during the era of hypercompliance. These interpretations pulled unfunded and exempt research projects into the orbit of the regulations, filtered through their most conservative reading. Later, however, a social movement among IRB and other research administrators promoted a more flexible approach, providing some researchers in disciplines like sociology and anthropology with much-needed relief.

Chapter 6 compares across three different varieties of compliance bureaucracy: EEO, IRB, and financial services. In all three fields, organizations hired compliance professionals to help them conform to complex and ambiguous rules. However, there was one revealing difference. Both IRB and financial services compliance offices came to embrace efficiency goals, as exemplified by the widespread use of compliance software and outsourcing to external vendors. In contrast, EEO offices did not adopt efficiency-enhancing innovations. I argue that this difference can be attributed to distinct varieties of compliance: those defined by a logic of confidence, assessed by courts that reward recognizable gestures of good faith; and those governed by a logic of auditability, assessed in regulatory inspections that place a premium on meticulously recorded procedural details. The relatively high cost of the latter creates efficiency pressures, which are reflected in the rhetoric and norms of compliance professionals.

In the conclusion, I revisit the major findings of the book, discuss the 2018 revisions to federal regulations governing IRBs, and contemplate the American model in the context of other national systems. Although the new regulations contained some significant changes, they did not represent a major departure from the system's workaround logic. There are numerous benefits to having a more centralized government role in human research protections, as illustrated by the British case. Yet in the American context, there may also be some advantages to a privatized system that provides protections beyond the reach of antiregulatory politics.

1

The Federal Crackdown and the Twilight of Approximate Compliance

"BOY, THIS WAS A WAKE-UP CALL," Alan recalled. "When we looked at headlines, we said, 'Wow, look what the government did! I wonder if we're in any jeopardy?'" (compliance office director, academic medical center). It was the late 1990s, and federal regulators were penalizing leading research institutions for failing to comply with the IRB rules. In 1998, Rush Presbyterian Medical Center was ordered to suspend its federally funded research with human subjects. In 1999, both the Duke University Medical Center and the Los Angeles Veterans Administration Medical Center were similarly ordered to shut down thousands of studies.

The federal crackdown that Alan remembered so vividly was triggered by shocking research scandals, a growing sense in Washington that the IRB system was broken, and mounting pressure on regulators to act. This chapter explores the deeper roots of the crackdown and analyzes the regulatory framework within which it occurred. IRBs were part of a workaround system—one that delegated decisions to local boards, relied on the labor of unpaid faculty volunteers, and was overseen by under-resourced offices located in hidden corners of the federal bureaucracy. This structure was a legacy of political obstacles to building a more robust system back in the early 1970s, when the National Research Act was passed, as well as hurdles to reforming the system in the decades that followed.

For many years, this structure functioned adequately enough. Yet, as the world of biomedical research became larger, more commercialized, and more complex, there was a growing disproportion between the enormous task apportioned to IRBs and the scant resources they could deploy to address it. This set the stage for an outbreak of research scandals—and for regulators to respond by disciplining errant research institutions. The crackdown would profoundly and permanently alter how IRBs approached their duties.

The IRB System in Brief

IRBs are on the front lines of two overlapping regulatory systems. Among academics, the better known of the two has jurisdiction over institutions that receive federal research funding, and is governed by the Code of Federal Regulations, Title 45, Part 46 (45 CFR 46), today usually referred to as the Common Rule. Compliance with the Common Rule is overseen by an office within the Department of Health and Human Services (DHHS), the parent organization of the National Institutes of Health (NIH). A second structure has jurisdiction over privately sponsored research, such as clinical trials financed by pharmaceutical companies. This system is governed by 21 CFR 50, 56 and overseen by the U.S. Food and Drug Administration (FDA), an agency also located within DHHS that in practice behaves quite autonomously. Many IRBs manage compliance with both the Common Rule (for federally funded studies) and FDA regulations (for privately funded studies).

These two sets of regulations rely on distinct enforcement mechanisms, reflecting the different powers of their respective enforcers. The office overseeing the Common Rule wields the power of the purse. Every institution receiving research funds from NIH (as well as from other federal agencies that are part of the rule) must sign a formal "assurance" that it will uphold the IRB policy: research with human subjects sponsored by these agencies must be reviewed by a duly constituted board following federal rules. Regulators can suspend the assurances of institutions found to be out of compliance—and thereby suspend their federally funded research.

In contrast, FDA's power lies in its ability to withhold its approval from drugs, biologics, and medical devices, and thereby keep them off the market. An applicant for FDA approval must report the name of the IRB that reviewed the research. FDA has the ability to suspend or disqualify an offending IRB's ability to review studies. The agency can also restrict, disqualify, or even criminally prosecute investigators if they fail to adhere to human subjects protection rules.[1]

The Common Rule and FDA regulations are nevertheless closely aligned. Under both, boards review research proposals to determine whether subjects are being put at risk, whether risks outweigh benefits to subjects, and whether they are being given the opportunity to provide informed consent. IRBs are also charged with conducting periodic follow-up ("continuing") reviews. Regulations require that IRBs have at least five members, including at least one "non-scientist" and at least one member not affiliated with the institution. Boards must follow prescribed regulatory procedures and file reports with federal agencies when research goes awry.

Such stipulations aside, IRBs exercise tremendous autonomy. The federal offices entrusted with their oversight are empowered neither to set precedents nor to accept appeals. It is a structure designed to delegate judgment to local boards.[2]

The Workaround Regulation of Research Ethics

The origins of this system can be traced back to the decades following the Second World War, a time of rapidly expanding funding for biomedical research. Most of this money was channeled through NIH, which began to require that its researchers submit their proposals for ethics review by a panel of their colleagues.[3] This became the official policy of NIH's parent agency, and was expanded to extramural researchers. The notion that ethics assessment should be conducted by a local group of professional colleagues spread and flourished, as federally sanctioned "institutional peer review committees" began to crop up around the country at hospitals and universities receiving NIH funding.[4] At around this time, FDA—which was housed with NIH under the roof of the same agency—began to require similar review of new investigational drug applications.[5]

This embryonic IRB framework was already in place when Senate hearings in the early 1970s revealed a shocking array of ethical abuses in biomedical research. In addition to the horrors of the Tuskegee syphilis study, there were many other examples, some of which included a clinical trial for birth control in which women were given a placebo without their knowledge, frontal lobotomies in psychosurgery research, and military cancer victims being treated with lethal levels of full-body radiation.[6]

In light of these blood-curdling reports, Congress sought to replace federal agencies' internal policies with more substantial oversight, and debated various alternatives. One bill introduced by Senator Hubert Humphrey (S. 934) proposed the creation of a powerful National Human Experimentation Board, similar to the National Labor Relations Board. The board would be empowered to pass regulations, set precedents, and "review all planned medical experiments that involve human beings which are funded in whole or in part with Federal funds." National board members would be paid federal salaries, and would be "persons of demonstrated knowledge, education, and experience in the field of clinical investigations" appointed by the president.[7]

Humphrey's National Human Experimentation Board would have set American human research protections on a centralizing trajectory, similar to what emerged in European countries many decades later.[8] This proposal quickly dropped out of Senate discussions. Subsequent debates focused on a second bill, proposed by Senator Edward Kennedy (S. 2072) that would have set up a permanent national commission with the power to promulgate and enforce regulations, as well as to certify local review boards. Unlike Humphrey's plan, the Kennedy option would have kept local IRBs in charge of reviewing NIH research. Nevertheless, it would have provided them with strong leadership and direction: a permanent expert commission with the authority to set the agenda for review boards across the country and to serve as a precedent-setting appeals body.[9]

Although a version of Kennedy's plan was made law in the National Research Act of 1974, the bill was significantly watered down in the process of political compromise. Although the law established a national commission, it was a temporary one with a purely advisory function. The act also authorized the promulgation of new regulations (45 CFR 46) that were practically identical to the old NIH policy and that would be overseen by the same small office within NIH. These regulations, along with all their subsequent iterations, were founded on two premises: the wholesale delegation of decisions to local boards financed by research institutions, and their oversight by subagencies located deep within the federal health bureaucracy.[10]

In hindsight, it is clear that more centralized federal governance of human research ethics was doomed by two features of the American political landscape. First, centralization was antithetical to the interests of powerful actors. The biomedical research community strongly opposed any potential imposition on their professional autonomy. In this, they had the backing of their powerful patron, NIH, which also preferred a decentralized system because it insulated the institute from legal problems and public controversy.[11]

Second, there was limited appetite among lawmakers for expanding state capacity in this way. Although Democrats controlled both chambers of Congress, House Democrats were warier of big-government solutions than their colleagues in the Senate.[12] Kennedy's original proposal was also strongly opposed by the Nixon administration. As one top health official explained at the time, the administration "wanted to try . . . to stop the continued federal intrusion into matters that were not properly the concern of the government."[13]

For liberal reformers during the 1960s and 1970s, such political limitations posed a perpetual dilemma, commonly addressed through a variety of workarounds, such as relying on private lawsuits for enforcement, or by devolving costs onto state governments.[14] In the case of human research protections, the solution was to build on the existing NIH policy, complete with its weak core and delegated decision making. This was the founding workaround of the IRB system—the compromise that enabled legislation and regulations to protect human subjects, but that would also lead to problems down the line.

The Era of Approximate Compliance

In 1974, the die was cast for the decentralized governance of human research protections, with regulations that replicated the delegated logic of the earlier NIH policy. In 1981, these regulations were updated to reflect some of the recommendations of the National Commission for the Protection of Human Subjects of Biomedical and Behavioral Research, and a similar set of FDA rules was issued. A decade later, in 1991, a long list of government agencies signed on to a third version of the 45 CFR 46 regulations, which became known as the Common Rule. A continuous theme running throughout these iterations was the outsourcing of ethical judgments to local committees with limited government oversight.

The evidence suggests that until the mid-1990s or so, IRBs complied with the regulations approximately. One former regulator recalled finding that "it seemed like a lot of IRBs . . . didn't pay a whole lot of attention to the letter of the regulations. You know, they were seen more as general principles rather than regulations."[15] This impression was echoed by other former regulators among my informants. At that time, IRB members were often guided by informal norms—their own habitual practices, or the practices of other boards—rather than by a close reading of the rules.

Such an imprecise approach was encouraged by a confluence of circumstances. For one thing, full-fledged compliance had become steadily more labor-intensive. The 1981 update to the regulations had marked a conceptual turning point, in which IRBs became something more than peer review committees. They were required to have at least one "non-scientist" member, and at least one member not affiliated with the institution. More significantly (for the purposes of this chapter), they were charged with more extensive regulatory and administrative responsibilities—to follow in detail the procedures spelled out the regulations, and to record that these procedures had been followed.[16]

With the transformation of internal policies into regulations, and with each subsequent update, these mandated procedures increased in volume and complexity. The 1981 regulations were over 10,000 words long, more than double the length of the 1974 version; the 1991 Common Rule, with its added subparts for pregnant women, fetuses, neonates, prisoners, and children, weighed in at more than 12,000 words. Each set of rules grew organically out of its forbears, and was rewritten by regulatory offices in stages with input from the National Commission, lawmakers, some civil society groups—and later, with the Common Rule, the many federal agencies that had to be cajoled into signing on.[17] Each layered new requirements atop the old.

The result was an intricate, overlapping set of decision criteria, subcriteria, and exceptions that could mystify even the most motivated faculty board member. To take just one example from the Common Rule, there were six categories of research that qualified for exemption. One of these six exemption eligibility categories was research "involving survey or interview proce-dures," which could be exempt *unless* subjects could be identified, *and* such identification could put the subject at risk, *and* the study dealt with "sensitive topics" such as sexual behavior or drug use—*unless* the study subjects were "elected or appointed public officials or candidates for public office," in which case they were exempted unconditionally. The regulations were also riddled with gray areas, where their meaning was subject to interpretation.

The potential for misunderstanding was magnified by regulatory fragmentation—the fact that IRBs were governed by an overlapping patch-work of rules, which included not only the NIH and FDA regulations, but also a host of other agency requirements and state-specific rules. As the Na-tional Bioethics Advisory Commission (NBAC) later charged: "The oversight system [is] unnecessarily confusing and open to misinterpretation. Not only do different rules apply to different research studies, but a single study may be subject to more than one set of regulations . . . IRBs and investigators are often uncertain which rules apply or to whom they must report."[18]

For all these reasons, following the rules required time and attention—both of which were in short supply during an era when IRBs were still mostly run on the side by faculty, with minimal staff assistance. These professor-volunteers might take their ethical duties very seriously, while paying less attention their regulatory obligations. In theory, their tendency to miscon-strue or neglect the rules might have been corrected by clear feedback from regulatory agencies. Yet in practice, regulators were stretched too thin to reliably provide such feedback.

At that time, the agency in charge of overseeing compliance with 45 CFR 46 was the Office for Protection from Research Risks (OPRR), OHRP's pre-decessor. Located within NIH, this relatively obscure office depended on the funding decisions of its parent institute, which seemed to consider it a low priority: with around thirty employees, OPRR had the job of overseeing not only the human research protections rules for thousands of academic insti-tutions, but also a separate set of regulations governing animal research.[19] This disproportion between mandate and resources was almost humorously extreme, as can be seen in an exchange between the office's director, Gary Ellis, and Representative Christopher Shays in a congressional hearing:

MR. SHAYS. Dr. Ellis, let me just ask you, how many professionals do you
have on your staff?

MR. ELLIS. Our office is about 30 people total, professional [and] support
staff. We oversee protection of human subjects and animal subjects in
research. I think you're probably most interested in professionals relating
to human subjects.

MR. SHAYS. So how many dealing with human beings?

MR. ELLIS. We have probably 13 to 16 professionals. I don't have the chart in
front me. We have support staff and professionals.

MR. SHAYS. How many investigators do you have dealing with human
subjects?

MR. ELLIS. We have one full-time professional and portions of two or three
other professionals.

MR. SHAYS. When you say that I have a certain feeling when I hear it, do you
have a certain feeling when you say it about the absurdity of it?

MR. ELLIS. Absurdity is your word. Meager might be another word, meager
resources given the effort.

MR. SHAYS. Maybe pathetic.[20]

Given these constraints, until the mid-1990s OPRR engaged in few investigations and almost no enforcement. Charles McCarthy, Ellis's predecessor at
the head of the agency, had embraced an educational approach to regulatory
feedback, which was less expensive than compliance monitoring and sanctions. McCarthy oversaw a series of regional programs designed to educate
researchers, IRBs, and institutions, which apparently enjoyed some success.
Yet even these interventions were not cost-free, and during the Reagan and
Bush administrations OPRR's education budget was whittled down to almost
nothing.[21]

The other overseeing agency, FDA, faced resource challenges of its own.
Although FDA did engage in regular inspections, its priority was consumer
safety rather than the protection of research participants. Responsibility for
overseeing IRBs at the agency was divided across several different offices,
none of which was dedicated specifically to the issue.[22] With federal agencies unable to regularly educate or enforce, faculty-run IRBs were often left

to their own devices, encouraging an inattentive, imprecise interpretation of complex regulations.

The Changing World of Biomedical Research

For about two decades, the IRB system bumped along, attracting little outside notice. Yet the research landscape was evolving rapidly, challenging the system with transformative changes. This created the conditions for a fresh wave of biomedical scandals, drawing the attention of federal watchdogs, public interest organizations, and members of Congress.

In the twenty years following the passage of the National Research Act, there had been an extraordinary expansion in research funding opportunities. On the one hand, there was a bonanza in federal money: between the mid-1980s and the end of the 1990s, the real-dollar value of the NIH budget more than doubled.[23] On the other hand, there was an even greater surge in commercial investment in trials for potentially profitable drugs, devices, and biologics. By the beginning of the 1990s, private investment in biomedical investigation surpassed that of NIH (see Chapter 4). A large and growing proportion of this research was outsourced to contract research organizations (CROs)—companies hired by pharmaceutical firms to identify sites for clinical trials, to broker contracts between sites and sponsoring pharmaceutical firms, and to monitor the resulting data. Often their studies were run by physicians who recruited their own patients or community members.[24]

At the same time, the boundary between academic and commercial research was blurring. A series of laws intended to create stronger ties between federally funded research and the private sector encouraged academic institutions to establish technology transfer offices, and to patent and profit from scientific discoveries in collaboration with private firms. These incentives had a particularly notable impact in the area of biotechnology, which attracted an influx of venture capital funds.[25]

Meanwhile, biomedical research was becoming far more complex. As knowledge accumulated, studies became more specialized—and their ethical issues more difficult to evaluate by local researchers lacking esoteric knowledge. Research was increasingly conducted not within the halls of a single university or academic medical center, but across multiple research sites.

These accumulating novelties were putting ever-greater strain on the IRB system, which had been designed for a simpler time. Washington began to notice. A series of government reports and congressional hearings raised the alarm, and concluded that the system was in need of a major update. As Connecticut representative Christopher Shays told a congressional subcommittee: "Today's research environment has changed dramatically. Institutional Review Boards have not."[26]

Most of the perceived problems were directly related to the system's reliance on local expertise, judgment, and resources. The scarce labor of unpaid faculty volunteers was observably inadequate to the explosive growth of biomedical research. "IRB members are usually physicians, scientists, university professors, and hospital department heads who are not paid for their IRB service," reported the U.S. General Accounting Office in 1996. "In some cases, the sheer number of studies necessitates that IRBs spend only 1 or 2 minutes of review per study."[27] Administrative staff could have relieved faculty board members of some of the burden. Yet at that time IRB staff were few in number, and often had only clerical qualifications. There were strict limitations on the administrative costs that could be charged to federal grants, and upper academic administrators did not always see spending on IRB staff as a budget priority, particularly at a time when many medical centers were struggling financially.[28]

These pressures were heightened by an epidemic of conflicts of interest. With growing commercialization, there was an enormous financial incentive to get clinical trials under way with all due speed. The regulations did not make IRBs responsible for monitoring conflicts of interest, but their proliferation—combined with IRBs' overwhelming workload and pressure to get research approved—made it more likely that ethical deficiencies would be overlooked.[29]

Finally, a system founded on local review was ill equipped to manage growing complexity. As research became more specialized, local boards found it more difficult to muster the needed expertise.[30] Studies that involved more than one research site, as were becoming the norm in the biomedical field, created headaches for IRBs and investigators alike when multiple boards arrived at different decisions about how to conduct the same study.[31]

The Federal Crackdown

In the spring of 1994, OPRR director Gary Ellis was called to testify to a subcommittee of the U.S. House of Representatives about the federal system for protecting human research subjects. "I know you are most concerned about the possibility that this system can somehow fail," he acknowledged. "I would characterize that possibility as 'slight.'"[32]

These comforting words notwithstanding, a new wave of biomedical research scandals was looming on the horizon. As Ellis made his testimony, researchers at the University of California, Los Angeles were being investigated for deliberately taking mentally ill patients off their medication to exacerbate their symptoms, sometimes leading them to suffer severe relapses. Two years later, in 1996, a research participant named Michele Wan died after being given a lethal dose of lidocaine in a University of Rochester clinical trial. In 1999, Jesse Gelsinger died after being given an experimental treatment without having received accurate information about its substantial risks.[33]

Publicity around these and other research misdeeds was generating public mistrust of the ethics of clinical trials—and political pressure to do something about it. Although this challenge was taken up by both OPRR and FDA, it was the former that had the most impact. This was because OPRR had the power to discipline institutions through suspending their assurances and halting their federally funded studies—a highly visible form of sanction that immediately drew the attention of research administrators across the country.

Under Ellis's leadership, the agency mobilized its meager resources and began to act. It stepped up its audits of research institutions and issued enforcement letters ("letters of determination")—publicly available documents that could damage institutions' reputations. In some egregious cases, OPRR used its most dreaded weapon: the temporary shutdown of federal funding through the suspension of institutions' assurances. The crackdown reached its crescendo around the turn of the twentieth century (see figure 1.1). Between 1998 and 2002, the agency suspended or restricted federally funded research at seven major hospitals and universities.[34]

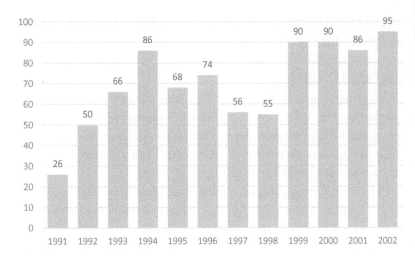

FIGURE 1.1. OPRR/OHRP compliance investigations opened, 1991–2002. *Source*: OHRP internal database supplied to fulfill Freedom of Information Act request.

This unprecedented show of federal force made an enormous impression. "Across the country, university administrators and researchers are worried, even panicked, that the same thing could happen at their institutions," observed the *Chronicle of Higher Education* in 2000, "with millions of dollars of research funds from the National Institutes of Health and pharmaceutical companies at stake."[35]

The main message of the crackdown—conveyed in hundreds of enforcement letters scrutinized anxiously by thousands of administrators and IRB members—was that approximate compliance was not enough. In some cases, institutions were reprimanded for incorrectly interpreting regulatory gray areas. In most instances, however, they had overlooked requirements that were spelled out in black and white. Among the most common citations were inadequate minute-keeping, improperly constituted boards, and inadequate written policies and procedures.[36]

Another recurring theme in these enforcement letters was the failure to "make findings"—to generate documentation to demonstrate that regulatory criteria for decisions had been considered. For example, IRBs were cited for waiving the requirement of signed consent documents—not because such waivers were prohibited, but because federal auditors could find no record that the board had found that the preconditions for such waivers had been met.[37] The mantra of regulators during the crackdown was "If it wasn't documented, it didn't happen."[38]

To some critics, there was a troubling disconnect between regulators' emphasis on process and paperwork, on the one hand, and their ostensible goal of protecting human subjects, on the other. "Some of the regulatory and paperwork requirements governing IRBs are difficult to interpret . . . , unnecessarily burdensome, and often not commensurate with their contribution to protecting research participants," complained one influential advisory body.[39]

In reality, however, these apparently trivial considerations were essential features of a system that depended on federal offices being able to review comprehensive records of local IRB activities.[40] Regulators had neither the mandate nor the resources to second-guess local boards' ethical decisions—to serve as a Supreme Court of IRBs. Instead, their job was to make sure that boards carried out the correct series of actions prescribed in the rules, and the only way they could make such determinations was through scrutinizing written records. Recognizing this, the 1981 regulations had introduced far more elaborate recordkeeping requirements than their 1974 predecessors.[41]

During the era of approximate compliance, as we have seen, these mundane details were often neglected on boards run by faculty, who were minimally interested in the regulations and struggling to cope with a growing workload. The federal crackdown clearly revealed, for the first time, that the routine, mass production of auditable indicators was at the heart of what it meant to comply. This lesson would not soon be forgotten.

The Failure of Reform

In response to systemic failures, OPRR used the tools it had available by disciplining institutions for faulty paperwork and procedures. To provide the office with greater autonomy from NIH, whose research it regulated, in 2000 OPRR was removed from its location within NIH, renamed OHRP, and relieved of the charge of overseeing regulations to protect laboratory animals.[42]

Meanwhile, lawmakers were able to consider more fundamental reforms.[43] Some especially thoughtful proposals came from the presidential advisory commission NBAC,[44] which made dozens of recommendations in a lengthy report. Among other things, it called for the creation of an independent National Office for Human Research Oversight, charged with overseeing and interpreting a new, unified set of federal rules applying to both federal and commercial studies.[45]

This proposal found a receptive audience in Massachusetts senator Edward Kennedy—who had argued a quarter century earlier, unsuccessfully, for more centralized federal oversight. Sponsored by Kennedy in 2002, the Research Revitalization Act (S. 3060) would have established an independent lead agency, charged with overseeing the entire IRB structure—including research under the jurisdiction of both FDA and OHRP—as well as promulgating, interpreting, revising, and enforcing new regulations. The bill also called for millions of dollars in new funding, both for the new agency and to improve local IRB function. Research institutions would, for the first time, be able to charge IRB expenses as direct costs on their federal grants.[46]

In addition to providing much-needed assistance to local boards, Kennedy's bill aimed to strengthen the system's core by putting a strong, unified agency in charge of setting standards that were clearer and more straightforward for local IRBs to manage. Just as importantly, by creating an elevated authority, the law would have introduced greater flexibility into an ossified regulatory regime. The Common Rule's subordinate location within the federal bureaucracy made it extraordinarily difficult to change, thwarting proposals for reform. It could not be revised by OHRP because it represented a sort of treaty among seventeen different federal agencies that agreed to sign onto the rule after nearly a decade of grueling negotiations.[47] Had it become law, Kennedy's bill would have removed this major source of systemic rigidity.

However, Kennedy's attempt to rationalize the system died in committee and was never debated on the Senate floor.[48] The reasons for its failure were undoubtedly similar to those that doomed his attempts back in the 1970s. A more robust regulatory regime ran counter to the interests of powerful actors—not just the traditional biomedical research community, but a newer private biomedical research industry with accumulating clout in Washington.[49] There were also political obstacles: both the executive and the U.S. House of Representatives were controlled by Republicans, unlikely supporters of a bigger government role in overseeing biomedical research.

By the end of the twentieth century, the world of biomedical research was growing by leaps and bounds, changing rapidly, and posing new ethical and regulatory dilemmas. Meanwhile, the American policy framework for overseeing the ethics of human participants was locked in place, stymied by its legacy of delegated judgment, scarce resources, and fragile, fragmented authority. There was widespread agreement that the system needed a major overhaul, but powerful structural impediments prevented this from occurring.

Yet, while the system resisted policy change at the top, lower on the regulatory pyramid a major transition was taking place, stimulated by the federal crackdown. The following chapter shows how the crackdown led research institutions to invest in a new profession that would become a major participant in the governance of human research protections.

2

Leaving It to the Professionals

AS A YOUNG MOTHER with a master's degree in social science, Claire was searching for a job when an unexpected opportunity arose. A university had recently gotten in trouble with federal regulators for "a really huge human research protection scandal," as she recalled (research administrator, research university). Unnerved by sanctions and bad publicity, the university wanted to ensure that no such disaster ever occurred again.

"They were looking for someone to basically start a human research protections program," Claire remembered, "because all they had previously was an IRB with a kind of paraprofessional person running it in a very clerical fashion. But she wasn't expert in any way on the ethical or regulatory oversight of human research." Claire made a photocopy of the regulations and read them on the flight on the way to her interview. "I guess I read them well enough to sound knowledgeable," she recalled with a laugh. "They took a chance on me when they hired me." In this way, Claire was propelled into a lifelong career in research compliance administration.

Eve, a trained nurse working in clinical trials administration, had a similar tale. "When I arrived in this position [as IRB director] it was a brand new position and the only person . . . was a secretary who had been doing it for thirteen years," she recalled. "And then I was brought in" (IRB administrator, research university). Over time, Eve's staff grew, as did their role in the review process. A decade and a half after taking the job, Eve was supervising ten staff members.

Among my informants there were many variations on these narratives of professionalization. Starting around the late 1990s, many well-educated individuals began to take jobs in IRB administration. They learned to be human research protection experts on the job. Many oversaw offices that would increase notably—and sometimes dramatically—in size. Along the way, they became pioneers in the creation of a new profession, complete with its own association, annual meetings, and certification exam.

In this chapter, I tell the story of how the federal crackdown created fertile ground for this successful professionalization project. The crackdown increased the risk of compliance failure, but left the meaning of compliance unclear. This gave rise to the era of hypercompliance: a period when research institutions protected themselves by going above and beyond the rules. The crackdown also created a vigorous demand for experts to interpret these rules, thereby allowing a nascent IRB profession to acquire a secure home in research institutions. Workers in this growing field joined a national network of experts in ongoing communication, generating a froth of new ideas about how to run IRB offices. Some of these coalesced into popular best practices that would come to define the meaning of compliance.

The Era of Hypercompliance

The federal crackdown came as a shock to many IRB members and research administrators—a revelation that they had either neglected or misunderstood their regulatory responsibilities. For decades they had complied approximately, apparently to no ill effect. Now they were suddenly called upon to attend closely to a host of intricate details, as spelled out in hundreds of federal enforcement letters. Failure to do so could have severe consequences, including the suspension of an institution's federally funded research.

To avoid this dreaded fate, research institutions rushed to "recouple"— that is to say, to more closely adhere to rules once followed approximately.[1] Recoupling can be a difficult and tumultuous process; and, in this case, the agitation was heightened because it was not entirely clear with what, exactly, institutions were expected to recouple. Local IRB offices anxiously sought clarification from regulators, but regulators did not always have the resources to provide clear, immediate directives. This was especially evident in the case of the Office for Human Research Protections (OHRP), the agency in charge of overseeing the Common Rule. "HHS [the Department of Health and Human Services] has not increased OHRP's budget in proportion to the office's increased scope of work," reported the General Accounting Office in 2001, "and the office has not been able to hire the staff it planned to because of the federal hiring freeze." Consequently, the agency had a backlog of uncompleted compliance investigations, and was unable to issue guidance to clarify important gray areas.[2]

Moreover, what little guidance there was could be confusing. For example, in a September 2003 letter, OHRP indicated that oral history was not under the jurisdiction of IRB review. This was in response to oral historians' argument that the interviews they conducted were not designed to contribute to "generalizable knowledge," and hence did not constitute "research" according to the regulatory definition. However, in December of that same year, OHRP seemed to backtrack, and provided a list of examples of different kinds of oral history projects, some of which should be excluded from IRB review and others included. No further clarification was ever offered.[3]

By raising the cost of noncompliance without clearly defining compliance, the crackdown created high levels of uncertainty among research institutions. In a 2002 article, former OHRP director Greg Koski noted that "a climate of fear [was] often resulting in inappropriately cautious interpretations and practices that have unnecessarily impeded research without enhancing protections for the participants."[4] Since research institutions could not be faulted for erring on the side of caution, they were becoming more rigid and conservative, a practice I refer to as "hypercompliance."[5]

"The pendulum swung to being conservative, to cover your butt," colloquially explained one IRB veteran (Sheila, compliance office director, research university). Research was reviewed far more meticulously, and a great deal more supporting documentation was demanded. Standardized application forms asked many more questions, and informed consent documents became longer and more detailed, often well beyond what the regulations required.[6] Some IRBs were observed to be reviewing activities that did not meet the federal definition of "human subjects research."[7] Some boards also became reluctant to use expedited review procedures, and put low-risk research through full board review.[8] Others began to hold exempt research to the same standards as expedited research—for example, by instructing researchers to use the same informed consent documents with the same standardized language.[9] And although only federally funded research was required to go through IRB, many institutions began, with regulators' encouragement, to voluntarily expand IRB review to all human subjects research whether or not it was federally funded.[10]

Researchers noticed the difference. Biomedical investigators were suddenly encumbered by more red tape, and unfunded social and humanities scholars suddenly needed IRB approval to begin their research (see Chapter 5). Complaints about "getting through IRB" became a staple topic of conversation among researchers across the country. Meanwhile, behind the scenes, an equally important reaction to the crackdown was taking place, as research institutions began to invest in the IRB profession.

Evidence of Professionalization

The word "professional" often evokes occupations that are famous for very high status, pay, and autonomy, such as American medicine. However, most sociologists who study professions have a much more flexible definition. In this view, professionals are simply workers whose knowledge enables them to secure higher pay and status than unskilled workers.[11] They include not only doctors and lawyers, but also paralegals, social workers, and insurance underwriters, along with hundreds of other occupations. Some professionals, such as certain medical specialists in the United States, are highly autonomous. Others, such as social workers, labor in large organizations and are beholden to bureaucratic rules.

Occupations become professionalized, in part, by convincing the public that they possess specialized expertise. This process of building public recognition typically involves the founding of a professional association. The nascent IRB profession used an established organization, Public Responsibility in Medicine and Research (PRIM&R), as a launching pad for its profession project. Between 1995 and 2005 the organization's national membership increased more than threefold, to over 2,000 members.[12] Professions also promote recognition of their expertise through creating standards for certification. True to form, in PRIM&R launched a Certified IRB Professional (CIP) exam in 2000.

Yet the success of any profession also ultimately depends on finding someone to pay for its services. After all, the everyday definition of "professional" is not only someone who has specialized knowledge (unlike the unskilled worker), but also someone who is paid to put that knowledge into practice (unlike the amateur).[13] It is this second definition we invoke when we talk about "leaving it to the professionals."

The importance of finding a paying clientele was particularly evident in the case of the IRB profession, which took over jobs that had once been done by unpaid amateurs—the faculty volunteers who had been running IRBs on a shoestring. Although the federal crackdown exposed the defects of the amateur IRB model, decision makers at research institutions were initially reluctant to solve this problem by hiring administrative staff. After all, volunteer-run boards were cheap; administrators were expensive. As an official from the Association of American Medical Colleges told the *Chronicle of Higher Education* in 2000, protecting research subjects "is a tremendously resource-consumptive activity. Institutions want to support it in every way, but coming up with the resources is not easy to do."[14]

Over time, however, this resistance was eroded. Three years later, an article in *Academic Medicine* noted that "many institutions have reorganized their IRB and/or compliance programs. . . . In cases where the institution was cited and human subjects research was halted, dramatic changes have been made, often involving large commitments of financial resources."[15] Former OHRP director Greg Koski similarly reported that "institutions have in many cases doubled and tripled their commitments of resources to their human subjects protection programs."[16]

Most of these resources were spent on staff, whose numbers increased most dramatically at academic medical centers. Just as important as the increased quantity of administrative positions was the upgrading of their qualifications. For decades, the administration of IRB offices had been considered to be secretarial work. In contrast, now institutions were hiring staff with more advanced credentials. In a 2007 survey of the IRB world, 83 percent of respondents had at least a bachelor's degree, with 29 percent having master's and 21 percent doctoral degrees.[17] In a breathtakingly short span of time, IRB work had become professionalized.

This transformation was enabled by the federal crackdown, but did not occur automatically: it was actively promoted by agents on the ground, who worked to persuade decision makers to invest in IRB offices. These agents included faculty IRB chairs seeking a reduction in their workload, research administrators who were disposed to emulate their peers at other institutions, and consulting firms that advised institutions on how to stay out of trouble with the feds.[18] Perhaps the most important champions of professionalization were IRB professionals themselves—who, once hired, could become internal advocates for further hiring.

Mobilizing Resources for Professionalization

The crackdown "put a little bit of awareness into Vice Presidents or Presidents or Chancellors of the organizations that having a program, knowing that it's compliant, [is] an actual business need, an operation as important as finance" (Juliet, compliance office director, academic medical center). One key function staff members could perform was to correctly produce and manage auditable indicators of compliance. In the delegated, decentralized IRB system, the job of regulators was not to set precedents, but to ensure that boards followed the proper procedures—that they were properly constituted, considered the mandated criteria, and so on. The only way to make such determinations was to review IRBs' documentation. As OPRR (the Office for Protection from Research Risks) director Gary Ellis reminded boards in 1999, "If it wasn't documented, it didn't happen."[19]

It was clear from federal enforcement letters that amateur IRBs were not attending properly to this function. One leading deficiency cited in these letters was missing or insufficiently detailed meeting minutes. Another was the failure to "make findings"—that is to say, to both review protocols according to the criteria spelled out in the regulations and to provide a written record of each criterion having been considered.[20] There was a growing sense among research administrators that mastering the regulations was too important to leave to the amateurs. "People started . . . to look at how this thing called IRB administration had been handled," Stephen recalled, "and realized that just dumping it on the side of somebody's day job was not enough to really meet the demands" (compliance office director, government agency).

Whereas filing paperwork could be carried out by clerical staff, correctly interpreting what documents regulators would want to see in an audit required considerably more skill. Not only were the regulations complex and ambiguous, but they were fragmented and inconsistent. For example, the Health Insurance Portability and Accountability Act[21] and the Common Rule had concepts that were similar but not identical, such as "de-identified" versus "anonymous" data.[22] Similarly, whereas under the Common Rule boards needed to report "unanticipated problems," U.S. Food and Drug Administration (FDA) regulations stipulated the reporting of "adverse events," which had a somewhat different definition.[23] The meaning of the regulations could shift over time, as regulatory agencies issued new guidance. In theory, the purpose of guidance was to clarify; in practice, it created yet another level of esoteric complexity in need of expert interpretation.

Knowledge of this difficult terrain was at the heart of the IRB profession project, and the purpose of the CIP exam was precisely to validate and enhance the status of this emerging area of expertise. Developed within PRIM&R and first administered in 2000, the 250-question exam primarily tested knowledge of the finer details of federal regulations and guidance—precisely the kinds of details that faculty volunteers were least likely to learn and remember. As co-founder Susan Delano explained, the exam was "not designed for IRB members or chairs. . . . This is for people engaged in the day-to-day activity of running an IRB or overseeing that function."[24]

The CIP exam quickly became a ubiquitous standard—a way that universities and medical organizations routinely gauged the qualifications of actual and potential IRB employees. By 2010, more than 1,200 individuals had received certification.[25] "People who hold the CIP credential are now recognized by employers as having the knowledge base necessary to help run

IRBs in a compliant manner," Delano explained. "Many job postings include a requirement or preference for CIP certification."[26]

The Diffusion of Best Practices

In the past, IRBs had been secluded islands, defined by local cultures and run by faculty volunteers. In contrast, the IRB professionals who took over after the crackdown had both the time and the motivation to bind these disparate units together into a common whole. As full-time workers in the human research protection field, they could throw themselves with enthusiasm into attending meetings, reading trade publications, participating in online forums, cultivating relationships with their peers, and trading best practices.

The professionalization of IRB work followed a pattern that is common among compliance experts in the United States. The government defines compliance unclearly and inconsistently. Uncertain about how to stay out of trouble with regulators and the courts, organizations turn compliance over to specialized workers. This, in turn, enables these groups to further their professional project by establishing a nationwide network, creating ideal conditions for the development and spread of organizational practices from place to place.[27]

In the IRB world, the organization at the center of this emerging network was PRIM&R, founded in the late 1970s as a forum for discussing ethical issues in biomedical research. For many years the organization's membership was mostly made up of biomedical researchers and bioethicists.[28] In 1984, PRIM&R incorporated a subsidiary organization specifically for compliance administrators, the Applied Research Ethics National Association (ARENA). As research institutions hired more IRB administrators, ARENA membership grew to dominate that of its parent organization, and in 2006 it was merged back into PRIM&R (see figure 2.1).[29] From that point forward, compliance administrators would continue to make up a majority of members.

PRIM&R contributed to the human research protection profession in many ways. It helped educate novice administrators in professional norms. For example, the organization sponsored sessions at its annual meeting, as well as online webinars devoted to training IRB staff members. It also served

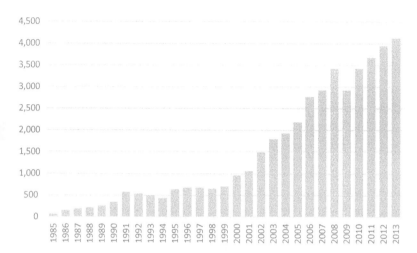

FIGURE 2.1. PRIM&R/ARENA membership, 1985–2013. *Source*: PRIM&R internal database.

as a sort of central headquarters for strategizing on behalf of the profession, as occurred with the development of the CIP exam.

Perhaps the most important contribution of PRIM&R was to bring individuals from across the country into communication with one another under the umbrella of a common occupational identity. This allowed ideas about managing IRBs to travel easily from place to place—from Berkeley to Boston and everywhere in between. Communication occurred on a PRIM&R-affiliated electronic discussion board, where IRB professionals could air their questions and problems to the community, and at the organization's annual meetings, where they could present at panels and poster sessions, sharing homegrown techniques for managing the labor of compliance. Many of my respondents felt that this was a leading benefit of attending the conference. For example:

> PRIM&R most often for me is walking out to find one really good session that just gives me a great idea for how I can come home and make things better here. . . . I get this one tidbit of knowledge and it's brilliant . . . it revolutionizes our IRB sometimes. (Gustavo, IRB administrator, research university)

At PRIM&R . . . I know that there are people there that I can go to and say,
"Hey! How did you guys do this?" (Erin, IRB administrator, research university)

The connections forged at these meetings could establish long-term professional relationships. More generally, PRIM&R fostered an awareness that
there were other workers struggling with similar problems at other institutions. This awareness in itself encouraged the borrowing of ideas from elsewhere. As Lara explained:

I'll absolutely go to our peer institutions or anyone we think is better than
us and grab whatever we can grab. . . . My favorites are Johns Hopkins,
Duke, Stanford, Harvard, Partners in Boston, and sometimes University
of Washington has really good stuff. (Lara, IRB administrator, research
university)

These ideas were commonly referred to as "best practices." This term had long
been popular in evidence-based medicine, where it referred to an industry
standard, based on the results of scientific studies.[30] But in the IRB world, its
meaning was somewhat more ambiguous, as Janice explained:

When I send my staff to [PRIM&R] conferences, I caution them. I say, "You
hear a lot of interesting things, and you probably will wonder how come my
office doesn't do it? I want to caution you that they are not requirements.
They're quote-unquote "best practices." (Janice, compliance office director,
academic medical center)

When I pressed Janice to define the term, she sighed: "I really don't know,
Sarah. . . . I think it depends on your institution. . . . It might not work for
another place."

Used in this sense, a best practice was in reality one of many good practices. It was a promising idea for how to run an IRB office—one that had the
potential to spread across institutions. "I think probably it's fair to say that
[we're] becoming more and more alike as people compare notes and share
best practices," remarked Stephen (research compliance director, government
agency). Not all best practices were equally good, but the most influential

ascended to the status of professional norms—widely shared assumptions about how work should be conducted.

The Professional Definition of Compliance

In an indirectly lit conference room, I sat in an audience of more than fifty people, mostly women in office-casual attire. Sitting in front of us was a row of five representatives from OHRP. This "Dialogue with the Feds" panel was being held at an annual PRIM&R meeting and was advertised as an opportunity to "hear from OHRP representatives about evolving initiatives, issues, and guidance," and to "ask questions of OHRP representatives." Toward the end of the session, audience members lined up behind a microphone to ask their questions.

To me, the answers from the federal panelists seemed singularly unhelpful. They often consisted of verbatim quotations from the regulations, and otherwise tended to be couched in highly qualified language. For example, in response to a question regarding the application of data protection standards, a panelist used such noncommittal phrases as "it *all depends*" and "it *seems* like it *may well be* perfectly appropriate to say." In at least two instances regulators on the panel appeared to disagree. And in response to a question about how to calculate informational risks, a panelist replied that "we're interested in learning the answer," and expressed disappointment that a PRIM&R panel on the topic had been canceled.

In this scene, regulators and human research protection professionals enacted a familiar drama in the world of American compliance. Regulators had limited capacity to clarify gray areas in the rules: not only were they overworked and understaffed, but they also lacked the authority to issue official precedents. To fill this interpretive vacuum, compliance professionals began to set standards, or "best practices" of their own.[31]

One of the profession's most visible standard-setting contributions was the Collaborative Institutional Training Initiative (CITI). Designed to train investigators and board members in research ethics and the regulations, this online program quickly became a dominant standard in the field. So ubiquitous did the course become that some investigators might have assumed that it was developed by federal regulators, or at least mandated by the regulations.

Neither was true. The course was officially sanctioned by neither OHRP nor FDA. It was developed not by federal regulators, but by a group of biomedical researchers and IRB administrators.

CITI originated in the kind of ambiguous federal directive that characterizes the workaround state. On May 23, 2000, Health and Human Services Secretary Donna Shalala announced that her agency would "undertake an aggressive effort to improve the education and training of clinical investigators, IRB members, and associated IRB and institutional staff."[32] From that point forward, institutions receiving NIH funds needed to have investigator training programs in place, and grant applicants needed to check a box indicating that they had received human subjects training. Yet the agency did not provide any further details about what such training should entail: as Craig recalled, "They simply said, 'You have to train.' They didn't say how" (compliance consulting firm, associate).

In response to this call, the CITI online education platform was launched at the end of that same year. Institutions that paid to subscribe could require that researchers present CITI certification as part of their IRB review materials. Although CITI was not officially connected to PRIM&R, human research protection professionals were leaders in the design of the platform's content and prominent on the organization's management and advisory board.[33]

CITI was an immediate success: by 2007, more than 600,000 individuals at over 700 institutions had acquired certification, with an increasing number in countries outside the United States (where U.S.-sponsored clinical trials were conducted).[34] Over time, CITI launched additional units, including courses not only for IRB members and investigators, but also in other areas of research compliance, such as clinical billing, information privacy, and laboratory animal care. Later the course was acquired by a private firm specializing in biomedical research support services.[35] In this way, CITI became one of many private vendors selling their wares on the human research protections marketplace (*see* Chapter 4).

The CITI platform represented a private solution to a long-standing problem: namely, that investigators often had very little knowledge of either research ethics or federal regulations, rendering their oversight by IRBs more onerous and time-consuming. In theory, investigator training could have been run out of a federal agency. Indeed, NIH did begin offering its own, considerably shorter, online tutorial in 2008. However, IRB administrators eschewed the NIH course in favor of the more comprehensive CITI platform, and in 2018 the NIH tutorial was eliminated, leaving research institutions, once again, to rely entirely on the private provision of human research protections training.[36]

During the federal crackdown, the regulation of research with human subjects was transformed by professionalization. Once run by faculty chairs with secretarial assistance, IRB offices were placed in the hands of credentialed experts. The most immediate need met by these professionals was to bring organizations into alignment with regulations that were both demanding and confusing. But very soon thereafter, an equally powerful rationale for professionalization began to emerge: the need to make IRBs not only compliant, but also efficient. This efficiency rationale is explored in the following chapter.

3

Organizing for Efficiency

IN 2003, Craig was hired to direct the IRB of a major research university, home to a large academic medical center that was struggling with a dilemma. On the one hand, it wanted to avoid the dreaded "poor review that would end up haunting us in the future because some regulatory agency would come across it and take a severe action against us," as Craig recalled (compliance consulting firm, associate). On the other hand, it needed to keep hypercompliant IRB policies from undermining millions of dollars of sponsored biomedical research. Researchers had been complaining that reviews were slow and capricious, and that beleaguered staff members were rude.

To solve these problems, the university doubled the number of IRB staff, and put Craig, an experienced administrator, in charge of reorganizing the review system. Once on the job, Craig retooled office activities around a far more elaborate division of labor: "Once a protocol came in [it was] treated like a car on an assembly line in Detroit," he explained.

This chapter is about the dawn of the era of compliance with efficiency. In it, I argue that the federal crackdown raised the cost of compliance to unacceptably high levels, and that this subjected IRBs to powerful pressures to become more efficient—particularly where there were large volumes of sponsored research at stake. The problem was addressed through the standard tools of bureaucratic administration: expert staff, a more complex division of labor, and a growing use of efficiency-enhancing routines.

This process, unleashed in IRBs across the country, was "rationalizing" in the Weberian sense. In German social theorist Max Weber's ideal bureaucracy, tasks were carried out by full-time salaried professionals who made their careers within the organization. This meant that officials had the time to learn a vocation in depth—they "by constant practice increased their expertise."[1] Because they carried out their duties according to written rules and an elaborate division of labor, more work could be accomplished with greater uniformity and speed.

Rationalization completed IRBs' transformation from amateur boards into compliance bureaucracies, and definitively shifted the locus of decision making from faculty volunteers to administrative staff. This transition had unintended consequences, such as increased friction between IRBs and investigators, and goal displacement, as upper administrators used IRB processes to pursue extraneous ends. Nevertheless, rationalization appeared to accomplish its intended objective of making reviews faster, more consistent, and less intrusive.

The Origins of the Efficiency Imperative

The era of hypercompliance was widely remembered as a time of profound dysfunction in the IRB world. "No one was happy," Owen recalled. "IRB administrators were overwhelmed and investigators were unhappy and research was delayed" (IRB administrator, research university). At that time, Diane recalled, investigators began to refer to IRB as "the black hole" or "the roadblock" (IRB administrator, research university).

These maladies were consequences of the risky environment created by the federal crackdown. On the one hand, hundreds of enforcement letters indicated that IRBs needed to focus more on the production of auditable compliance indicators: extensive documentation that federally mandated procedures had been followed. On the other hand, because regulators' signals were ambiguous and inconsistent, there was still widespread confusion about what compliance entailed. This caused IRB offices to go above and beyond the rules, just in case.

The production of auditable hypercompliance was labor-intensive and created multiple levels of obstruction to the research process. Boards once accustomed to following the rules approximately now struggled to consider intricate lists of decision criteria and painstakingly document that each had been followed. Faculty volunteers were encouraged to scrutinize research proposals more carefully, to ask more questions of investigators, and to layer on more conditions for approval. This led to inconsistencies and delays in IRB decisions, putting valuable sponsored research at risk. It also meant that faculty board members were spending an inordinate amount of their valuable time on IRB service.

Meanwhile, auditable hypercompliance was consuming more of investigators' time. Application forms mushroomed in size, as IRB offices sought to more diligently detect risk and to document that sufficient information had been gathered to make compliant decisions. A 2005 study found that IRB paperwork and delays were among the top regulatory burdens reported by sponsored researchers.[2]

In response to this dismal state of affairs, research institutions and IRBs began to expand from focusing exclusively on avoiding compliance risk to considering how to reduce compliance cost—a thematic shift marking the move into the era of compliance with efficiency. The emerging consensus—among investigators, research administrators, and research sponsors alike—was that the review process had to be made more efficient. Craig recalled "a movement . . . to increase the efficiency of IRBs . . . particularly on the bio-medical side where there's been criticism on the clinical trials starting too slow." "There was a clear call from sponsors, from NIH, from industry for better efficiency," Edward confirmed (compliance office and IRB director, academic medical center).

Enabling this quest for efficiency was a gradual improvement in the regulatory climate. The crackdown was coming to an end. Federal offices were starting to behave in a less disciplinary fashion, as evidenced in a long-term decline in OHRP (Office for Human Research Protections) enforcement letters starting in 2003. During the George W. Bush administration, the office was placed under the directorship of Bernard Schwetz, who adopted a conciliatory, educational approach similar to that of Charles McCarthy years earlier.[3] The research scandals of the 1990s were fading from public memory—and, in any case, federal agencies did not have the means to keep research institutions on a short leash for very long. As Schwetz explained in an interview: "We are not out there checking every investigator, every study. We don't have the resources to do that."[4]

The Impact of Accreditation Standards

One reason federal regulators were standing down was that the gears of a new, private regulatory mechanism had started to engage, following the 2001 founding of the Association for the Accreditation of Human Research Protection Programs (AAHRPP, pronounced "ay-harp"). Accreditation was supported by policy makers and regulators as a way to achieve more intensive oversight without putting additional strain on meagerly resourced federal offices: it would be financed not by taxpayer dollars, but by research institutions paying accreditation fees. The new organization was backed by the nascent IRB profession, as well as by top medical research administrators, who felt that regular visits from a private accreditor were preferable to reputation-damaging federal audits.[5] Once founded, AAHRPP quickly drove a competing accrediting agency out of business, and rose to become the leading standard setter in the IRB world.[6]

AAHRPP's growing influence had far-reaching consequences for the IRB world, two of which are particularly relevant for this chapter. First, AAHRPP became a leading apostle of the new efficiency gospel, which it spread across the country through its accreditation standards (discussed at greater length in chapter 4). "I think IRBs have spent a lot of time in the last few years trying to put all the policies and procedures in place to have a program that's compliant with the regulations," explained AAHRPP's director in 2005. "I think once they have a system in place that meets federal regulations, then they can begin to address questions around efficiency."[7]

Second, accreditation standards saddled IRB offices with an even heavier load of administrative labor. Like federal auditors, accreditation site visitors looked for scrupulous adherence to the letter of the regulations. Unlike the feds, however, AAHRPP pursued goals beyond mere compliance—taking to heart a motto often repeated during the federal crackdown, that the regulations were "a floor, not a ceiling." Whereas a federal auditor would want to see well-kept records, an AAHRPP site visitor would expect them to be painstakingly pristine. While regulators expected boards to have written policies and procedures that conformed to federal requirements, AAHRPP wanted these to be far more elaborate and detailed—perhaps even absurdly so, as critics sometimes complained.

Membership in the AAHRPP club therefore entailed a great deal of work. In addition to the everyday demands of running an accredited office, there was the work of preparing for site visits, which recurred every three years after the initial approval and involved an astonishing level of effort. "It's the biggest pain in the ass I've ever lived through," Amy remarked of her recent accreditation experience, "and you don't recover from it, ever" (IRB administrator, research university). Accreditation created a further rationale for investing in compliance bureaucracy, since such demanding labors could not conceivably be carried out by faculty volunteers, or even by a small IRB staff. This burden, combined with the high cost of the accreditor's fees, meant that it was a large but elite minority of research institutions that earned accreditation: those that managed large numbers of sponsored biomedical studies and could afford the requisite level of staffing.

Routinizing the Review Process

In response to the efficiency imperative and accreditors' demands, research institutions launched a second wave of investment in professional staff. At institutions administering many large biomedical grants, the size of IRB offices could swell to ten, fifteen, or even more, and job ladders were created to encourage staff to invest in long-term compliance careers within the organization.[8]

In contrast to the first wave (described in chapter 2), which was designed to lessen compliance risk, the second wave sought to lower the high cost of compliance. One leading cost was the time and effort investigators were putting into navigating the IRB process—an artifact of tightly coupled hypercompliance. "When the IRB office just got too slow . . . leadership finally decided it really was a matter of staffing, then we got additional staff," Nicholas remembered (associate, compliance consulting firm). Kimberly similarly recalled that around 2005, there was a decision to hire more staff "to handle the volumes so that people weren't waiting endlessly for their IRB approval" (IRB administrator, research university).

To remove undesirable obstructions to the research process, IRB offices used the standard tools of bureaucratic administration—organizational routines that allowed them to regularize output, minimize discretion, and accomplish more work using the same amount of labor.[9] These routines were introduced through standard operating procedures (SOPs), or step-by-step rules for carrying out the daily activities of an IRB office.[10] Typically, SOPs would be drafted by an IRB or compliance office director with input from other upper-level administrators, and approved by a body with faculty participants, such as a faculty senate or convened board.

Over time, SOPs became extremely detailed, especially at AAHRPP-accredited institutions. For example, in 2017 the accredited Northwestern University IRB had thirty-eight SOPs. The following is an excerpt from the SOP for staff members' "daily tasks":

5.1 Check for individuals whose training is not through the CITI training program and will lapse in the next 30 days, and complete and send "TEMPLATE LETTER: Training Reminder (HRP-531)."

5.2 Check for emergency uses where the IRB has not received a report, within 5 days:

    5.2.1 Complete and send "TEMPLATE LETTER: Failure to Submit Emergency Use Report (HRP-551)."

    5.2.2 Consider placing the principal investigator on the Restricted list.

    5.2.3 Process the failure to submit as a Finding of Non-Compliance under "SOP: New Information (HRP-024)."

5.3 Check for individuals whose training has lapsed:

    5.3.1 Complete and send the "TEMPLATE LETTER: Failure to Undergo Training (HRP-554)."

    5.3.2 Consider placing the principal investigator on the Restricted list.

    5.3.3 Process the failure to submit as a Finding of Non-Compliance under "SOP: New Information (HRP-024)."

    5.3.4 If the individual is an IRB member, follow "SOP: IRB Membership Removal (HRP-083)."[11]

Routines affected each of the three types of reviews spelled out in federal regulations. Full board reviews, as the name implied, were those brought to the convened board; they were reserved for the riskiest cases or those that involved special populations, such as prisoners. Expedited reviews were for research defined as minimal risk and were handled by a smaller number of qualified reviewers. Exemption (from IRB review) was technically not a review category, but came to strongly resemble one during the federal crackdown (see Chapter 5); its criteria overlapped confusingly with those of expedited review, and it was supposed to be for low-risk research that warranted the least amount of scrutiny.

One of the most important routines to be adopted was "pre-review:" the practice of having one or more staff members screen a protocol (as proposals submitted to IRB review were called) before forwarding it to the next level of decision making. Pre-review was particularly important for streamlining full board decisions. "Before the pre-review process was instituted, the board never approved anything," recalled Eve, exaggerating for effect. "And the meetings were five hours long and they had five pages of changes that had to be [made by the principal investigator]" (IRB administrator, research university). Staff pre-reviewers were charged with identifying potential problems in a protocol and asking the investigator to make changes—for example, to add more information, or to change the wording in an informed consent form. Pre-review simultaneously sped up the process, reduced the workload for faculty volunteers, improved consistency, and ensured that the regulations were rigorously upheld.

Pre-review could prevent the dreaded "tabling" of protocols—the bête noire of every IRB office. A tabled protocol was one that had been brought to the convened board, only to be set aside for consideration at a later meeting, which might not occur until weeks or even months later, to the great aggravation of the investigator. Usually the reason for tabling was that the initial protocol contained insufficient information—for example, the investigator failed to provide a description of her recruitment procedure, which meant that she would need to be contacted for further information. Pre-review could forestall this possibility by cleaning up obvious problems before protocols went to the board, all the while ensuring that important regulatory criteria were not being missed. By the time a protocol appeared before the board, it would already be vigorously screened and cleaned, making it possible for board members to focus exclusively on ethical issues. "The board is sort of the recipient. The 'end user,' so to speak, of the study," Andrea explained (administrator, independent IRB).

As IRB offices became more rationalized, they adopted routinizing devices known as "tools" in the IRB trade, including forms, templates, and checklists. Tools performed an important compliance function: they ensured that fussy regulatory minutiae were not overlooked by serving as "cognitive nets" that forced attention to detail.[12] "The regulations are complex," Stephen explained. "I think the idea behind the checklist was to acknowledge that it's probably false to think that all IRB members and reviewers have these things all memorized by heart" (compliance office director, government agency). Templates and forms served a similar purpose—for example, an informed consent template could ensure that investigators included the federally mandated "elements." Just as importantly, tools created a paper trail of auditable compliance indicators. As Stephen put it, "If OHRP does come to town, or FDA [the U.S. Food and Drug Administration], if you've got a checklist that shows if somebody went down and checked off eight criteria, you can say you did your job." Forms, templates, and checklists were often couched in language lifted directly from the regulations, which meant that they could be filed as part of the auditable record.

Tools were not only useful for guaranteeing compliance; they could also improve efficiency. Standardized forms were quicker for IRB decision makers to process. Consent templates lessened the time spent by staff on corresponding with investigators. Checklists accelerated decision making and allowed IRB offices to make full use of nonexpert labor: armed with a standardizing checklist, even an entry-level staff member or an inexperienced faculty reviewer could be entrusted with important regulatory work.

Routinization was enhanced by the introduction of electronic protocol management software, which came to partially or fully supplant stand-alone tools.[13] Forms, templates, and checklists were subsumed within electronic systems, which were touted as time-savers by the vendors who sold them. "Quickly create, submit, or approve applications, consent forms, and other study documents," advertised one leading firm.[14] As they increased in sophistication, electronic platforms offered a growing array of labor-saving functions—for example, automatically forwarding completed forms and supporting documents to different levels of review.

Electronic systems were therefore used to control the burgeoning financial cost of running IRB offices. According to one 2007 study, the median price tag for running an IRB office at an academic medical center cost was over $700,000, with staff salaries the leading expense.[15] Electronic systems could help reduce this cost by automating clerical functions, and IRB offices across the country reported that they were facilitating the elimination of lower-level staff positions.[16] None of my respondents expressed regret about this trend. Rather than filing, photocopying, and distributing paper, the remaining IRB staff could now focus on higher-status tasks, such as following trends in regulatory guidance, updating local policies, and educating researchers.[17] By phasing out clerical work, electronic systems became an important enabler of professionalization.

Shifting the Locus of Decision Making

On the amateur board of the past, faculty chairpersons had been in the driver's seat, with staff riding shotgun. In the post-crackdown world, IRB professionals took their place behind the steering wheel and began to make important decisions. Experienced staff took the lead in interpreting regulations and designing policies and procedures; increasingly, they became voting board members.[18] As IRBs became more rationalized, staff members also took charge of a host of routine judgments that I refer to as "everyday decisions."

Under the rationalized IRB model, reviews were broken into component decisions governed by organizational rules, in a structure that resembled a factory. At the end of one assembly line were full board reviews—the most visible part of the IRB process, and the one in which faculty decisions played the greatest role. In other parts of the factory, however, a host of less glamorous, more routine decisions had to be made. The more thoroughly rationalized the IRB, the more it delegated everyday decisions to staff, in three major arenas. First, staff were almost always in charge of determining whether a study qualified for exemption, or what changes an investigator would need to make in order to so qualify.[19] Second, staff were increasingly placed in charge of expedited reviews, which the regulations allowed if they became board members.[20] Having staff participate in this realm helped IRBs respond to efficiency pressures, as Alan explained:

> We utilize a lot of our IRB administrators to perform expedited reviews. . . . It used to be more on the volunteers, but it's become too overwhelming . . . you've got to figure out a way to reduce the workload, so we do everything in this office to reduce the workload of our faculty IRB members. (Compliance director, academic medical center)

Third, and as described earlier, staff were in charge of "cleaning up" protocols in the pre-review process, before they came to the board—a practice that unburdened faculty board members and decreased approval times. The pre-review process typically involved multiple everyday decisions—for example, regarding the adequacy of a consent document, or privacy protections to subjects.

Everyday decisions were typically heavily circumscribed by routines: SOPs, checklists, and other tools designed to maximize consistency and minimize discretion. For example, figure 3.1 is an excerpt from a checklist designed for expedited reviewers. Such tools made it possible for everyday decisions to be given to less experienced staff (or to faculty volunteers lacking regulatory knowledge). Yet even when governed by routines, everyday decisions could contain a large element of discretion. For example, figure 3.1 illustrates how an expedited reviewer would need to decide whether a study was "minimal risk."

The discretion that inhered in everyday IRB decisions was directly related to ambiguities in the federal regulations. For instance, the Common Rule defined "minimal risk" as meaning that "the risks of harm anticipated in the proposed research are not greater . . . than those ordinarily encountered in daily life or during the performance of routine physical or psychological examinations or tests." Yet this apparently precise definition belied the subjective element inherent in assessing future risks, in balancing the magnitude with the probability of risk, or in assessing difficult-to-measure social or psychological risks.[21] Such ambiguities, which might have been at least

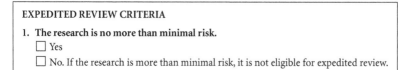

FIGURE 3.1. Excerpt from Expedited Reviewer Checklist, Research University. *Source*: West Virginia University Human Research Protections Office. Reprinted with permission.

partly clarified by a more powerful regulatory authority, were often left to local authorities to work out for themselves.

The "minimal risk" designation was one of many judgment calls that could fall to an everyday decision maker. Other examples included: whether risks were reasonable in relation to benefits; whether selection of subjects was equitable; and whether adequate provisions had been made to protect the privacy and confidentiality of subjects. A particularly difficult judgment was assessing subjects' "vulnerability." According to the 1991 Common Rule, an IRB needed to determine whether "some or all of the subjects are likely to be vulnerable to coercion or undue influence, *such as* children, prisoners, pregnant women, mentally disabled persons, or economically or educationally disadvantaged persons" (emphasis added).[22] This passage, which was replicated in the 2018 update to the Common Rule, neither defined the meaning of "vulnerable to coercion or undue influence" nor exhaustively enumerated examples of the concept, leaving open the possibility that other kinds of subjects might be considered vulnerable—for example, gay men and lesbians, college students, or military personnel.[23] The regulations stated that vulnerable subjects should be protected by "additional safeguards," but failed to specify what these safeguards might be. This meant that an everyday decision maker might have to decide whether a proposed research population was vulnerable—and, if so, what to do about it.

These routine decisions could be highly consequential for investigators and for research institutions. If an everyday decision maker overestimated risk and added too many protections, it could make research unfeasible; yet underestimating risk could put institutions in regulatory, legal, or reputational peril. Everyday decisions thus placed IRB offices at a vortex of conflicting currents, leading to unintended consequences.

The Dilemma of Bureaucratic Authority

Although rationalization was widespread, not all IRBs became equally rationalized. Boards at biomedical research institutions were subject to strong efficiency pressures, and developed highly elaborated bureaucratic structures. For-profit independent IRBs, whose business model depended on conducting compliant reviews quickly and meticulously, were famously routinized and efficient (as discussed in Chapter 4). In contrast, anecdotal evidence suggests that liberal arts colleges often maintained a more old-fashioned style of board, with modest secretarial assistance and relatively underdeveloped policies and procedures. Not only did such colleges have more limited resources to invest in compliance administration, but they had scant incentives to do so: with little sponsored research and small numbers of protocols, their risk of receiving a federal audit was vanishingly small.

For the institutions that embraced it, rationalization was the leading strategy for controlling the high organizational and financial cost of compliance. An indirect indicator of its success could be found in a decline in publicized complaints from biomedical researchers (as described in publications such as the *Chronicle of Higher Education*), which tapered off notably after the early 2000s. For these researchers, the system appeared to be functioning more efficiently. We will see in chapter 5 that social and humanities scholars did not experience the blessings of efficiency in the same way, since they faced their own distinct array of problems with the IRB review process.

Rationalization also had unintended consequences. One was the creation of tension between collegial and bureaucratic authority. For most of the history of the IRB system, this tension was muted or nonexistent, because boards were collegial entities dominated by faculty decision makers.[24] After the 1981 update to the regulations, boards were required to have nonacademic members and to maintain staff "to support the IRB's review and recordkeeping duties." Yet neither lay members nor clerical staff in a supportive role posed a significant threat to collegial authority.[25] It was not until well-credentialed

staff members acquired the ability to make consequential decisions that frictions began to arise. The abrasion occurred not between IRB staff members
and faculty board members—by all accounts, faculty volunteers were grateful
for the reduction in workload and regulatory responsibilities—but between
staff and investigators.

IRBs were charged with making decisions that could be unpopular with
the researchers who were supposed to abide by them. The legitimacy of these
judgments was enhanced by their appeal to collegial authority—the idea they
were being made by fellow investigators. As two social scientists contended in
a 2007 article, "*IRBs are faculty-run committees*. If tenured faculty account for
the majority of IRB members and the governance processes of the institution
are functioning, then the protection of human subjects and the maintenance
of academic freedom should not be at risk" (emphasis added).[26]

Yet even as these words were published, it was no longer strictly accurate
to describe IRBs at large research institutions, much less for-profit independent IRBs, as "faculty-run committees." Faculty did continue to play a key
role in full board reviews, but as we have seen, convened board judgments
were now just the tip of a much larger iceberg of decision making. Investigators were not oblivious to these changes: many had a growing sense that
their research was being governed by local rules and everyday decisions.
In theory, such decisions were contestable: according to the regulations, a
research protocol could be disapproved only by a convened IRB. In practice, however, the structure of bureaucratic decision making gave everyday
reviewers considerable gatekeeping authority. An everyday reviewer could
fail to approve an expedited protocol, to register an exemption, or to forward a protocol to the next level of review. An investigator seeking timely
IRB approval had a strong incentive to make the changes requested by the
reviewer, particularly if her institution lacked a mechanism to make appeals
in such cases.[27]

This sometimes put staff in the unenviable position of responding politely
to angry faculty members. "Occasionally, someone will criticize, complain,
or even yell at an IRB staff professional," reported a 2013 article in a trade
journal. "It happens, and IRB staff should learn how to handle these conflicts
without taking them personally."[28] Sometimes a disgruntled investigator might

question a staff member's interpretation of regulations. As Sharlene lamented: "One of the problems I have is with researchers who read the regs. They're professors. . . . They know all these things. So they read the regulations, and make up their mind. And when they're wrong, it borders on noncompliance" (IRB director, research university). The crux of the problem, however, was not regulatory expertise, but rather the unwillingness of scholarly experts to accept nonacademic authority over their research design:

> An issue we struggle with . . . trying to get my staff . . . empowered to do the IRB reviews completely themselves . . . [is the] credibility issue. "So how come you've got a staff member . . . telling me that I should do my research here or not?" And that's a delicate line to tread. (Sheila, compliance office director, research university)

In response, staff members sometimes invoked collegial authority by suggesting that they were merely anticipating the wishes of faculty board members, as a number of my respondents mentioned:

> This doesn't look like it would fly with our [faculty] reviewers. (Laura, IRB administrator, research university)

> The board isn't going to accept that argument for the minimization of risk. (Erin, IRB administrator, research university)

> Knowing how our IRB [faculty] chairs have viewed this in the past . . . it would be better if you [do] not get a written informed consent. (Sheila, compliance office director, research university)

The Dilemma of Goal Displacement

A second unintended consequence of rationalization was goal displacement—the adoption by an organization of new goals not included in its original mandate (sometimes known as "mission creep"). The concept was first described a century ago by sociologist Robert Michels in a study of the German Social Democratic Party in the early twentieth century. The party was originally dominated by member-volunteers, but lost its amateur character over time because it was simply too difficult for volunteers to administer the increasingly complex, burdensome tasks that the organization needed to carry out. As Michels explained, in such cases "the members have to give up the idea of themselves conducting or even supervising the whole administration, and are compelled to hand these tasks over to trustworthy persons specially nominated for the purpose, to salaried officials."[29]

What Michels ultimately sought to explain was the loss of revolutionary fervor in a socialist party, and there are limitations to the analogy. But his general observation that salaried officials can shift the goals pursued by an organization is relevant to the case here. Whereas the old-fashioned IRB was a collegial body beholden only to distant federal regulators, the new bureaucratic IRB was firmly located under the jurisdiction of upper administration (see figure I.1 in the introduction), which could use an IRB to pursue goals other than the protection of human subjects. Pressure for goal displacement could emanate from various locations, including university legal departments and other administrative offices. One key pressure point was the "institutional official"—an IRB manager's administrative superior who signed off on the assurance of regulatory compliance and whom one informant described as "the final deciding vote" on important IRB decisions (Laura, IRB administrator, research university).

A relatively benign example of goal displacement was the use of IRBs to manage other regulatory processes, such as radiation safety, conflict of interest, or data protection. Some IRB administrators were uncomfortable with these added duties: "Sometimes we're the gatekeepers for these other ancillary committee processes . . . that have to happen before the research ultimately gets initiated," Tanya remarked. "And that's a lot of responsibility in an IRB. It's more than . . . their charge" (compliance office director, research university). "[IRBs] are a central point of contact with investigators," Elizabeth explained. "It's an easy target . . . a good place to put another stop and say, 'Well, when it comes in for IRB review, let's not approve until we have all these other things checked out, too'" (compliance office director, research university). This could create headaches for IRB staff, since researchers would inevitably blame them for the delays in getting their protocols approved.

A perhaps more troubling form of goal displacement was the use of IRBs to engage in institutional protection—to shield their organizations from either legal liability or reputational damage. I was surprised to find that my informants openly acknowledged this practice and sometimes saw it as a commonsense part of their jobs. For Edward, the IRB office had

> a dual role. The primary role, of course, is to ensure that the subjects are protected and that the approval criteria are met. But there are sometimes . . . additional concerns. . . . Maybe the approval criteria can be met, but it's not something . . . our organization would feel comfortable with either because of reputational issues, or because of a potential legal issue. (Compliance office and IRB director, academic medical center)

Madeline recalled an undergraduate student who proposed interviewing drug dealers; the research was disapproved because it was considered to be too dangerous to the student researcher. In Madeline's view, "The whole IRB operation operates according to the [regional newspaper] rule; you don't want it to appear in the headlines. So we need to worry about the protection, about the participant, the researcher, and the institution" (IRB administrator, liberal arts college). Other respondents used very similar language:

> One of my jobs is to keep us out of the *Washington Post* and *New York Times*. It's just one of my jobs. I'm not supposed to let my boss get blindsided. . . . And so when I see a protocol that's about something funky, I call him. (Sharlene, IRB administrator, research university)

> I'm worried about what's going to show up on the front page of the [regional newspaper], that somebody is going to be suing the institution and we didn't even know about it. (Jean, IRB administrator, research university)

One informant mentioned that her university had an ancillary committee that reviewed IRB protocols for their potential impact on the university's reputation: "I think that when we review protocols, it's not just looking at the individual subjects, but also at the research outcomes, and how the public may view them. . . . I wouldn't say it's at the forefront, but I would say there's a sensitivity there" (Diane, IRB administrator, research university).

Goal displacement could create problems for IRB staff, investigators, and even research participants. The best known problem was the ballooning length and complexity of informed consent documents—which defeated the purpose of informed consent, since participants were less likely to read or understand them. The bloating of informed consent was widely understood in the IRB world as resulting from institutions' efforts to protect themselves from lawsuits.[30] As one bioethicist observed: "Almost everybody recognizes that shorter and simpler are better, but there remain some very strong influences that I personally think have to do with liability. This keeps consent forms much longer than anybody . . . thinks is appropriate."[31]

The impulse toward institutional protection also led IRB offices to adopt and maintain "site permission" policies, requiring a researcher to get an official letter of permission from an organization whose members were being studied. Site permission was not a regulatory requirement, and had far more to do with institutional protection than protecting human participants. Indeed, some informants explicitly defended their site permission policy as a means of protecting the institution from legal liability and reputational damage:

> To be honest, it's not a human participant issue because it doesn't really matter to human participants whether we get [site] permission. . . . It's a researchers' safety issue and institutional issue, really. If research gets published and it's clear that it was done at [particular] locations, and the subject of the research was somehow sensitive, then it could become an issue. (Maria, compliance office director, research university)

> It's more of a courtesy thing for us—the IRB spends a lot of time trying to minimize risks or problems, but they're not always risks to subjects. They may be institutional risks. (Sophia, IRB administrator, research university)

> We don't want there to be a bad impression. (Vivian, IRB administrator, health care network)

The requirement of site permission could be particularly problematic in a research location where organizational authorities could act against participants' interests. Such authorities might have an interest in silencing the views of proposed subjects—for example, managers of a factory might deny an investigator's petition to study a labor movement there.[32] Organizational authorities alerted to the presence of a researcher might even do the subjects harm, as in a case Laura described:

> Site permission is definitely a weird one. We had a person go over to another country and they wanted to interview people outside of a police station and talk about . . . their interactions with the police state. . . . And he was like, "If I have to involve the police station . . . I'm kind of asking for more trouble."
> (IRB administrator, research university)

Caught between the high risk of compliance failure and the high cost of compliance, research institutions sought to lower the cost. Rationalization allowed them to reduce the burden on faculty volunteers, to lessen the intrusion on biomedical research, and to rein in the expense of running IRB offices. Although it had unintended consequences, rationalization transformed many IRBs into well-oiled, protocol-processing machines, and marked the rise of a new epoch: the era of compliance with efficiency.

Meanwhile, and in notable contrast, rationalization was conspicuously absent at the level of government policy. The federal framework that governed these boards remained the same flawed system that had been described throughout the 1990s as inadequate to the demands of modern biomedical research and that had stubbornly resisted reformers' attempts to change it. In fact, the rationalization of local boards could be seen precisely as a consequence of the failure of enlightened policy reform. Rationalized compliance bureaucracies allowed the biomedical research enterprise to control costs that were directly related to the system's incurable maladies. The system was costly because its rules were fragmented, confusing, and imperfectly clarified; because it delegated decision making and administrative work to local institutions; and because it incentivized meticulous, labor-intensive proceduralism. The rationalization of IRBs was a logical adaptation to an illogical system.

4

Ethics Review, Inc.

I WAS IN A CAVERNOUS EXHIBITION HALL, making my way along rows of convention booths. The most prominent belonged to Public Responsibility in Medicine and Research (PRIM&R), the sponsor of the conference. Two smaller and more inconspicuous tables were staffed by federal agencies. A majority of the exhibitors, however, represented private companies.

In contrast to the austere, uninviting federal regulators, the private stalls were adorned by large, colorful banners with eye-catching slogans. A software vendor claimed to be "the game changer for investigator-initiated protocols." A leading consulting firm declared that it could "reduce turnaround times by up to 60%." And a well-known independent IRB promised "daily IRB meetings to support your timelines." Most were also giving away free souvenirs, each sporting a company's logo and contact information, including pens, keychains, computer screen-cleaners, tote bags, notebooks, and water bottles. Baskets of free candy were strategically placed for passers-by to sample.

This scene powerfully illustrated the growing influence of private firms in the IRB world. In this chapter, I argue that during the first two decades of the twenty-first century, the human research protection field became "industrialized." I use this term to refer to the rise of an identifiable line of business in compliance services—a market niche colonized by specialized organizations that provided new employment options for IRB professionals.[1] Industrialization was accompanied by an overall movement toward the practices, rhetoric, and norms of private industry, including an assembly line–like division of labor and the appropriation of the language and symbolism of industrial management.

The impact of industrialization was uneven, and was most visible in IRBs reviewing commercially sponsored biomedical research. Yet standards set in the most industrialized sector spread throughout the human research protections world, fueled by the forces of market competition, accreditation, and professionals' inclination to borrow widely accepted best practices. This profoundly reshaped the human research protection field in seemingly irreversible ways.

The Commercialization of Biomedical Research

Once upon a time, biomedical research in the United States was dominated by government money. The scandals leading up to the passage of the National Research Act (such as the famous abuses of the Tuskegee syphilis study) were all the more scandalous because they had been financed by American taxpayers. The 1974 regulations required institutions to put studies funded by the National Institutes of Health (NIH) through IRB review.

As the decades passed, however, biomedical research became dominated by profit-seeking firms. By the late 1980s, the budget of NIH was outstripped by the research investment of leading pharmaceutical companies (see figure 4.1). According to a study in the *Journal of the American Medical Association*, by 2006 fewer than 15 percent of clinical trials being registered in the United States were funded by NIH and other U.S. federal sponsors.[2]

The increased importance of commercial research dollars had profound implications. It revolutionized the way clinical trials were organized, gave birth to new organizations, and forced old ones to adopt new ways. It even penetrated the walls of the ivory tower: academic institutions began to establish profitable partnerships with private firms, stimulated by legislation designed to promote "technology transfer."[3]

Commercial studies were also increasingly carried out at nonacademic sites, such as local clinics and community hospitals, overseen by contract research organizations (CROs)—a large and growing sector of private companies that ran biomedical studies for pharmaceutical and other firms. CROs served

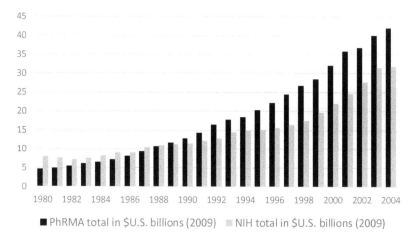

FIGURE 4.1. Research financing, privately sponsored pharmaceutical (PhRMA members) vs. NIH, 1980–2004. *Sources*: PhRMA website; NIH Almanac.

as brokers: they did not conduct research directly, but managed logistical details on behalf of the companies that hired them. They located sites, negotiated contracts, and monitored studies for data quality. CROs' success depended on their ability to deliver quick, competitively priced results to their clients. In this cutthroat environment, it often made sense for them to use nonacademic sites, which competed among themselves to provide timely, economical research results.[4]

Among the leading beneficiaries of these trends were independent IRBs, allowed for decades by the U.S. Food and Drug Administration (FDA). Just like NIH, its fellow agency within the same federal department, FDA had been dogged by scandal and public criticism during the 1960s and 1970s. In response, in 1971 FDA began to require that studies be reviewed by an IRB, but only if they were carried out at institutions with pre-existing boards; studies at sites without an IRB did not need to be reviewed.[5]

The problem was that FDA had borrowed its ethics review model from NIH—a model organized around the delegation of authority to place-based institutional committees. Unlike the academic studies funded by the institute, the commercial research overseen by FDA often occurred in places where there were no local boards available. A solution to this problem was offered in the preamble to the 1981 FDA regulations, which presented two options in such cases: studies could either be given to an existing board at a research institution; or to a board "created under the auspices of a local or State government health agency, a community hospital, a private or public medical school, a county or State medical society, the State medical licensing board or an IRB created by the sponsor."[6] Independent IRBs grew out of this indeterminate escape clause, and expanded to fill the market niche created by the expansion of commercial biomedical studies conducted outside the boundaries of academic institutions.

The Rise of Independent IRBs

Although technically not "institutional" (they were not attached to any particular institution), independent boards adhered to exactly the same regulatory requirements as their academic counterparts. As for-profit entities, independent boards charged for reviews. According to my informants, a typical base cost would be around two or three thousand dollars, with extra fees for additional services, such as amendments and the reporting of adverse events.

This injection of the profit motive into the ethics review process was troubling to some observers. Some worried that CROs, sponsors, and principal investigators could engage in "IRB shopping"—giving their business to the independent board that promised the least amount of hassle and thereby encouraging all such boards to be more lax in their standards.[7] This concern was lent credence by a federal sting operation that led to the closing of a small independent board in Colorado. The board had approved research containing significant risks omitted from the informed consent document.[8]

Yet it was also clear that compared to their academic counterparts, independent boards had many advantages. Because they were not locally based, they could draw on a much wider base of expertise, hiring specialized reviewers as needed for unusual studies.[9] They were faster, offering protocol review times that were about a third of those of traditional boards—a natural adaptation to the world of private pharmaceutical research, where there was great pressure to get drugs and devices approved and to market as soon as possible.[10] Particularly as the industry became consolidated, independent boards developed notable economies of scale: they could have very large staffs, typically including a team of attorneys, a highly specialized division of labor, and cutting-edge protocol management software to produce auditable compliance indicators on a grand scale. Independent IRB review was "a little bit like a factory. It's very efficient" (Frances, executive officer, independent IRB).

The larger independent boards thus achieved a steadily closer approximation to the Weberian ideal type of bureaucracy—a formal structure with an elaborate division of labor, run by paid expert officials. There was no such thing as a "faculty volunteer" on an independent board because all "scientist" members were compensated for their services. The role of collegial authority was highly circumscribed: with the exception of chairpersons, faculty serving on independent boards typically made decisions exclusively on matters requiring scholarly expertise. One informant close to the industry told me that a leading independent board had even replaced their faculty IRB chairpersons with administrators.

Independent boards also had an enormous advantage in the area of multisite research—studies carried out across multiple locations rather than at a single site. Traditional IRBs were famous for arriving at disparate decisions regarding a single multisite study, leading to significant hassle and delay—a dysfunctional legacy of the NIH system's delegation of authority to local institutions.[11] However, FDA rules offered a workaround solution: they explicitly allowed reviews to be contracted out to external boards, meaning that a single, independent IRB could assess the ethics of a study that was being carried out in many different places. Independent boards became famous for their skill at carrying out single reviews of clinical trials that sometimes spanned dozens of locations, a practice long common in private pharmaceutical studies.

The last frontier to be conquered by independent IRBs was the world of federally sponsored research regulated under the Common Rule. Although the use of external boards was not explicitly prohibited in federal studies, it was constrained.[12] Limitations on how expenses were charged to federal grants prevented them from being used to pay independent IRBs' substantial fees. Academic institutions worried that the Office for Human Research Protections (OHRP) would hold them responsible if an independent board made a mistake—a concern lent credence by some of the office's regulatory decisions. For these reasons, it seemed preferable to keep the review of federally funded studies in-house.

Over time, however, as the regulatory climate improved, these barriers to using independent boards for federal studies began to disappear. In the absence of renewed research scandals, federal agencies' attention had swung away from preventing ethical abuses toward removing impediments to life-saving research. And one glaringly apparent obstruction was the dilemma of divergent local IRB decisions in multisite studies. This problem now had an obvious solution, on full display for federal agencies to observe: single reviews of multisite studies, of the sort that were already being skillfully managed by independent IRBs for commercial sponsors.

In 2010, with uncharacteristic directness, OHRP explicitly indicated its support for single IRB review. "We recognize there can be inappropriate administrative burdens by having multiple reviews, and that can slow down research," explained the office's director, Jerry Menikoff. To solve the problem of institutional liability, the office made clear that it would be the IRB, rather than the research institution, that would be held responsible for any deficiencies found in a review. As Menikoff put it, "if something inappropriate happens in the study due to an outside IRB, whether it's a central or some other IRB doing something wrong, and we take a compliance action related to that, we will certainly make it clear in our findings that the fault was due to the IRB and not to the people in the institution."[13] Six years later, NIH began not only to encourage, but to actually require, single review for multisite studies—a mandate that would soon be echoed in the revised Common Rule.[14] Significantly, that same year the institute began to permit applicants to charge IRB review expenses as direct costs to their grants, thereby facilitating the use of NIH funds in paying independent IRB fees.[15]

Of course, the move toward single IRB review did not necessarily mean review by for-profit independent boards. There were nonprofit models available—for example, at the U.S. Department of Veterans Affairs and the National Cancer Institute. Academic institutions could engage in "reliance" agreements to designate one board as the single IRB of record.[16] Nevertheless, independent boards had long experience in carrying out multisite reviews and had all the comparative advantages described above.

The success of independent boards in winning over the business of first commercial and later federal sponsors made them quite profitable. Independent boards first proliferated, and then consolidated, as they were acquired by venture capital firms. For example, Schulman IRB was sold to Imperial Capital Group in 2008. In 2013 Western was brought into the WIRB-Copernicus Group, along with several smaller boards, under Arsenal Capital Partners.[17] Several years later, Chesapeake and Schulman IRB merged to form Advarra.[18] As Alan remarked wistfully: "I wish I had been smart enough twenty years ago to start an independent IRB like some of my friends did . . . they've made a lot of money" (compliance director, academic medical center). By 2016 it was estimated that independent IRBs were overseeing 70 percent of U.S. trials for drugs and medical devices.[19]

The Commercialization of Academic IRBs

Among IRB professionals, opinion about independent boards was divided, sometimes contentiously so. Informants from academic boards often felt that independents had a fundamental conflict of interest. "It's in their own economic interest to approve studies," complained Charles. "And if they're seen as a difficult IRB to a sponsor or someone who's paying for that IRB review, they're going to go somewhere else" (compliance office director, research university). IRB professionals with ties to independent boards, in contrast, argued that market pressures made them more rather than less scrupulous about ethics and compliance.[20] "There's zero incentive to do something wrong," Frances argued. "Because if you do something wrong, then you basically ruin your business" (executive officer, independent IRB).

Yet the distinction between the motivations of independent and traditional IRBs was less clear than it appeared. Academic boards were unexpectedly competing with their independent counterparts, and adopting some of their business practices as a result. This competition emerged as academic administrators increasingly allowed studies to be outsourced to independent boards as part of a strategy for courting commercial research money. After the late 1990s there was a precipitous fall in academic institutions' share of commercial studies—a particularly worrisome trend at a time when Congress was cutting back on federal research funding.[21] Partly driving the exodus of private money were the defects of academic IRBs, which had become especially slow and cumbersome in the wake of the federal crackdown and which struggled to reconcile decisions in multisite studies.

Academic administrators deployed an array of strategies to entice privately sponsored research to return. They hired consulting firms, emulated
the practices of CROs, and cultivated relationships with private sponsors.
And with encouragement from FDA, they began to outsource the review of
privately sponsored research to independent IRBs. According to one industry source, in 2010 about half of academic medical centers were outsourcing
industry-sponsored studies almost exclusively to independent boards.[22]

For traditional IRBs in the biomedical field, the growing use of independent boards posed an existential dilemma. When local investigators chose
to have their studies reviewed elsewhere, it weakened local boards' claim on
organizational resources. More immediately, it could decrease the revenue
they collected from application fees. The practice of charging fees became
popular during the federal crackdown—a time when increased federal regulatory demands had not been accompanied by a more generous flow of federal
resources to help meet them. "Is your IRB charging for reviews yet? If not,
you are probably in the minority," proclaimed a trade journal in 2003.[23] In
2006, a leading manual for IRB administrators advised that "charging an IRB
review fee for commercially sponsored research is a common way for an IRB
to supplement the operating budget provided by the institution. Sponsors do
not object to paying reasonable IRB review fees, and the additional revenue
can be used by the IRB to improve the quality and efficiency of its service."[24]

Over time, however, a growing share of this revenue was being diverted
to independent IRBs. This exposed academic and other local[25] IRBs to "if not
competition, at least comparison to the [independent] IRBs," as Judith put
it. "We're expected to operate in the same way" (IRB administrator, research
university). Janice similarly reported that investigators were explicitly com-
paring between the services provided by academic and independent IRBs:

> The pressure continues in terms of faster IRB turnaround time. . . . An aca-
> demic IRB asks too many questions. This is my cancer trial, other IRBs didn't
> have questions, how come your IRB has so many questions? Ridiculous, stupid
> questions. So more and more . . . institutions, they contract out to independent
> IRBs to process their protocols. Partly so that they could continue to attract
> those big pharma, their clinical trials to be done at their institution. . . . So in
> order to be competitive, to continue to attract pharmaceutical companies . . .

[there are] a lot of pressures on the IRB Office. (Compliance office director, academic medical center)

In response, some academic boards began to seek to replicate the efficiencies of their independent brethren, as Edward reported:

We looked at what [independent] IRBs were doing that were so good because everybody loved, you know, from the sponsored [research] end, the [independent] IRB model, so we said, Why is it that they have what we don't have? And we found out that they have a lot of boards and we found out that they meet very frequently, and that is the key to their efficiency. So that's exactly what we did. . . . We split our boards into eight boards instead of four. . . . Each board meets every other week instead of once a month. So now we have an IRB meeting every Monday, Tuesday, Wednesday, and Thursday. (Compliance office director, academic medical center)

In this way, the practices of independent IRBs spread to traditional boards through the forces of market competition. Competition among boards also began to alter the structural position of biomedical investigators—from involuntary objects of regulation into fee-paying clients, who could exercise choice in an IRB marketplace. A new discourse of "customer service" entered the lexicon of *both* independent *and* local boards, as evidenced in the following quotes from administrators interviewed for a trade publication:

We put a lot of effort into turning paper around and providing service to investigators. (Academic IRB, 2007)[26]

[We provide] a high level of service to investigators and [maintain] a good level of communication so as to minimize delays in all parts of the process. (Academic IRB, 2009)[27]

Our entire focus [is] on improving turnaround times and customer service. (Independent IRB, 2014)[28]

The Role of Private Accreditation

A leading beneficiary of both the commercialization of clinical research and the rise of independent IRBs was the Association for the Accreditation of

Human Research Protection Programs (AAHRPP). Founded in 2001, AAHRPP certified the quality of a client's "human research participant protection program"—a concept meant to encompass not only the tasks carried out to comply with the IRB regulations, but also a broader array of protective and compliance functions.[29] Rather than selling policy templates, the accreditor encouraged clients to find their own ways of achieving a list of standardized outcomes, more than 100 pages in length and publicly available on its website, along with numerous "tip sheets."

Accreditation was voluntary, and was acquired by only a minority of research institutions, for a number of reasons. For one, it was notoriously labor-intensive. To apply, IRB offices needed to submit a detailed self-assessment along with a massive amount of documentation. There would then be a site visit lasting two to four days, followed by a report from the accreditor detailing required changes, a response from the institution, and a final accreditation determination. Maintaining accreditation status also entailed a significant burden of administrative labor, as discussed in chapter 3.

For another thing, accreditation was very expensive. By 2017, the base fee for an organization overseeing up to 100 active protocols was $12,500; at the upper end, organizations overseeing 7,001 protocols or more paid $87,700. This was not a one-time cost; to maintain accreditation, institutions needed to pay a significant annual fee and to renew their status every three to five years.[30] Adding to the overall expense, many institutions relied on the services of private consulting firms to prepare for accreditation, and often purchased expensive new protocol management software as part of the process. The Huron Consulting Group was particularly well known for marketing its "accreditation readiness" services and software.[31]

Because the cost was so high, institutions that self-selected into the accreditation club tended to be those with high volumes of biomedical research. These were the institutions most likely to attract a federal audit, and also those most dedicated to attracting sponsored research dollars. As biomedical research became more commercialized, the client base for accreditation expanded to nonacademic research sites, such as community hospitals.

For the institutions that could afford it, the leading benefit of accreditation was that it signaled to regulators and sponsors that an IRB was scrupulously compliant. "Being accredited by AAHRPP signifies that you have a compliant human research protection program," explained one former site visitor, "that you . . . go above and beyond the minimal regulatory requirements" (Janice, compliance office director, academic medical center). Federal regulators, institutions hoped, would be less likely to audit an accredited organization. Indeed, OHRP's 2009 guidance on compliance oversight procedures listed "status of accreditation by professionally recognized human subject protection program accreditation groups" as a criterion for audit selection.[32]

The gold seal of accreditation became an especially important signaling device for independent IRBs. Despite their many competitive advantages, independent boards were vulnerable to being seen as less legitimate than their traditional IRB counterparts. AAHRPP accreditation, with its reputation for relentless rigor, provided a ready solution to this problem. In 2009, Pfizer became the first pharmaceutical company to be awarded AAHRPP accreditation, and the company announced that it would do business only with institutions that used AAHRPP-accredited IRBs.[33] By 2016 all the major independent IRBs were accredited.[34]

Accreditation occupied the corner of the IRB world most directly impacted by private money and market competition. This shaped the character of accreditation standards, the overall thrust of which was to combine rigorous regulatory review with speed and consistency. Thus, the value-added of accreditation was that it signaled not only ethical and regulatory probity, but also an IRB's ability to get clinical trials up and running with all due speed. As AAHRPP advertised in a brochure: "Industry sponsors, government agencies, and other funders recognize that accredited organizations have more efficient operations, produce high-quality data, provide more comprehensive protections, and strengthen public confidence in their organizations."[35] As part of the accreditation process institutions typically adopted a host of routinizing tools (see chapter 3), such as checklists and cutting-edge electronic systems.

Accreditation also committed organizations to regularly assessing and updating their policies and practices through "continuous quality improvement"—an industrial management philosophy that had become popular in the health care sector.[36] To meet AAHRPP quality improvement standards, institutions conducted periodic internal audits to assess various indicators of compliance, such as meeting minutes. It also kept tracking logs and performance metrics on indicators of such matters as how long it took for protocols to get approved. "Our quality improvement activities revolve around questions of efficiency and questions of quality," explained an administrator in a 2014 interview. "Metrics indicate it has made a noticeable difference, resulting in a shorter submission to review time."[37]

Accreditation standards were both a visible emblem of regulatory good faith and a marketing tool to potential clients. Accredited organizations literally displayed the AAHRPP "gold seal of approval" on their websites. When organizations adopt standards for such symbolic reasons, they often serve little functional purpose—they become "window dressing," as organizational sociologists sometimes call it.[38] AAHRPP standards were clearly not pure window dressing. After all, using the metrics gathered by clients, the accreditor could demonstrate that its certified IRBs were processing protocols with increasing speed.[39]

Such efficiency benefits notwithstanding, the extraordinary measures taken to meet these standards sometimes appeared to veer into more symbolic territory. An accredited organization might invest hundreds of person-hours to devising hundreds of pages of standard operating procedures (SOPs), including SOPs for developing new SOPs.[40] A larger accredited office might devote multiple staff members to new AAHRPP-inspired functions. For example, one independent board reportedly devoted seventeen employees to its "regulatory affairs and quality improvement team."[41] Such extremes were not universally viewed as functionally efficient. "The level of esoteric detail that gets forced on through some of the standards . . . make[s] you question the value added," admitted Stephen, who had once worked at an accredited IRB (compliance office director, government agency).

Yet even when the efficiencies were more rhetorical than real, accreditation was nevertheless performing its intended function. After all, the point of acquiring the gold seal was less to *become* more compliant and efficient than to acquire a *reputation* for compliance and efficiency. If accredited institutions sometimes went overboard as a result, it only served to bolster the accreditor's notoriety—and hence the value of its credential.

Accreditation standards were extraordinarily influential. As this book neared completion, there were fewer than 300 fully accredited institutions listed on AAHRPP's website, compared to more than 10,000 current assurances registered with OHRP.[42] Yet the accreditor's standards spread far and wide, because the IRB world had become a "field"—a densely connected network of individuals and organizations in the same area of social life.[43] At PRIM&R's annual conference, attended by IRB professionals from across the country, accreditation standards were on full display. Officials from AAHRPP were regular presenters at didactic workshops, and sometimes had their own stand-alone sessions. IRB professionals from accredited institutions shared their experiences at poster sessions with titles such as the following:

Using Lean Methodology to Improve the Implementation of a Web-Based IRB Submission System

Quality Assurance without Carrots or Sticks: Using Feedback Loops for Good Clinical Practice Audits

Improving Quality through Comprehensive IRB Staff Training for Taking IRB Meeting Minutes[44]

The intensely connected nature of the field meant that accreditation standards could travel from the high-flying world of commercial biomedicine to the most remote corners of the IRB world. For example, Ellen was the sole full-time staff member overseeing an academic board that mostly reviewed unfunded social and humanities research. There was no chance of her university paying accreditation fees. Nevertheless, Ellen regularly consulted AAHRPP's online tip sheets, and had even attended one of its annual conferences. As she explained, "It's great to share the standards of accreditation even if you don't pay the $15k it costs. It's like, why not? So it's like reaching for the best rather than reaching for the good. If that makes sense" (Ellen, IRB administrator, research university).

Over the course of the first two decades of the twenty-first century, the IRB field took on the characteristics of a private industry. Industrialization was driven both by the commercialization of biomedical research and unsolved dilemmas of policy. The once-intractable problem of multi-site research was addressed not by improved statutes or regulations, but by for-profit IRBs unweighted by the ballast of local review requirements, and honed to efficiency by market forces.

In the industrialized IRB world, for-profit independent boards vied for clientele by offering speedy turnaround of geographically dispersed proposals, while old-fashioned, local boards strove to keep pace—all assisted by a bevy of vendors offering specialized compliance services. To certify that market incentives were not corrupting the process, boards adopted the uncompromising standards of a private accreditor. Meanwhile, the field became permeated by a distinctly managerial discourse, complete with metrics, continuous quality improvement, and customer service. It was a spectacle as extraordinary as it was idiosyncratically American.

5

The Common Rule and Social Research

IT WAS THE FALL OF 1995, and I had just moved to a sunny apartment in Mexico City, where I would be doing research for my doctoral dissertation. I wanted to study the role of economists in Mexico's recent free-market reforms, but had not yet developed a clear research question. Overseeing my study—in the loosest possible sense—were three faculty committee members back home at Northwestern University. With the help of a Mexican mentor I began to conduct exploratory interviews with economists and public officials. Over time, these interviews became part of the research for my doctoral dissertation and first book.

Like most sociologists of my generation, I was not aware of the existence of IRBs when I was in graduate school. Indeed, I was already a tenured professor at Boston College when I submitted my first application for exemption from IRB review in 2005. This initial encounter was relatively painless, but soon thereafter I began to hear from graduate students about their problems "getting through IRB." I was also hearing similar stories from my colleagues at other institutions. In spite of these common encounters, it was difficult to identify the source of the problem. After all, the Common Rule that was causing headaches in 2005 was the same Common Rule in place when I was a graduate student ten years earlier—when it had affected me not at all. How could the same regulations have had such different consequences?

In this chapter, I argue that these remarkably distinct experiences were produced by two factors: a system that left the interpretation of the rules up to local institutions, in ways that were both intended and unintended; and the variable regulatory climate that informed those interpretations. During the balmy era of approximate compliance, institutions imbued complex, ambiguous rules with their most liberal reading. In this view, most social sciences and humanities research was either outside the scope of the regulations, exempt from its more onerous provisions, or both.

I conducted my doctoral research during the tail end of this golden age, but a more inclement regulatory climate was already on the horizon. During the federal crackdown, research institutions scrambled to comply with regulations that they did not completely understand. This led to the widespread adoption of hypercompliant local policies, designed to inoculate institutions from any possibility of risk.[1] Such policies pulled unfunded and exempt social research into the orbit of the Common Rule and subjected it to the rule's most conservative interpretation. The resulting experiences were immortalized in a generation of social researchers' IRB "horror stories."

However, this chapter also traces the more recent emergence of a friendlier IRB regime for social research. As the regulatory climate improved once again, there arose a movement advocating for a more flexible interpretation of the rules. Backed by accreditors and diffused by IRB professionals, flexibility norms spread across the country, offering relief to many social and humanities researchers. The movement's innovations were subsequently endorsed by federal regulators, in a powerful illustration of federal authorities embracing standards developed outside the state.

The Widening Dominion of the Common Rule

During the federal crackdown, regulators raised the cost of noncompliance without clearly explaining exactly what it meant to comply. As we have seen in earlier chapters, administrators and IRBs responded to this uncertainty by adopting hypercompliant policies that left nothing to chance, two of which became widespread and would have significant consequences for social and humanities researchers.

The first was to apply the Common Rule to unfunded research. Institutions did this in their assurances of compliance—official forms in which institutions pledged to uphold the Common Rule as a condition for receiving federal research funds. These documents contained a box that an institution could check or leave unchecked; "checking the box" indicated an institution's commitment to adhere to exactly the same requirements for all research with human subjects, irrespective of whether it was receiving funding from Common Rule signatories.

Checking the box was a voluntary decision, albeit one that was actively encouraged by federal regulators during the crackdown.[2] At a time when institutions were uncertain about what regulators wanted, taking the non-compulsory step of checking the box seemed like a prudent way to signal their good faith. As more institutions took this step, its appeal undoubtedly increased, since failing to check the box might expose an institution to unwanted regulatory attention. When institutions checked the box, they pledged to apply the IRB regulations to studies that did not have federal funding—a category that included the vast majority of social and humanities research.

The second widely adopted policy was to disallow researchers from determining whether their research was "exempt" from the regulations. Exemption was applicable to low-risk research that fell into a list of five categories, including "survey or interview procedures." As described in the work of historian Zachary Schrag, the introduction of the exemption category in 1981 was seen as a victory by social scientists fighting to avoid being swept up in the regulatory net in the years after the promulgation of the first IRB regulations. Although the exemption category was preserved in the 1991 Common Rule,[3] regulators subsequently issued guidance recommending that researchers not be allowed to determine whether their own research was exempt. At the height of the crackdown, such guidance was taken far more seriously than ever before, and exemption decisions were given over to IRB administrators.[4]

During the era of hypercompliance, this led to a hollowing out of the exemption category. IRB offices adopted risk-avoidant standard operating procedures that treated exemption determinations as little different from expedited review.[5] It became typical to require exemption applicants to submit not only a form describing the research, but also significant supporting documentation, including recruitment flyers, interview scripts, and informed consent documents. In theory, this was meant only to allow IRB decision makers to determine whether the research qualified for exemption. But in practice, it meant that IRB offices were increasingly asking researchers to modify elements of their exempt studies. Exemption from IRB review had become, for all intents and purposes, an IRB review category.

The Impact on Social and Humanities Research

These local responses to the federal crackdown—checking the box, and IRB review of exempt research—had far-reaching implications for scholars in disciplines like mine. It pulled us into the embrace of a regulatory system that we found baffling and sometimes maddening.

Our frustrations grew partly out of a mismatch between the way we did our work and federal rules built around experimental research designs.[6] As anthropologist Rena Lederman put it, "the federal system, through local IRBs, [incline] toward applying one homogeneous ethical standard, based on one concept of 'best practice': a highly idealized model of the 'scientific method' abstracted from clinical biomedicine and experimental behavioral research."[7]

The Common Rule and its forebears were premised on a system of prospective board review—one that presupposed that research would proceed in a predictable fashion that could be described comprehensively at the outset. Investigators were expected to submit a detailed description to the board for approval before research could commence. This worked reasonably well for an experimental researcher testing a hypothesis under controlled circumstances. However, qualitative researchers almost never started out with hypotheses, but rather with broad questions that evolved in unpredictable ways, following an inductive style of inquiry.

For example, when I arrived in Mexico to do my dissertation study, I did not have a clear research question, much less a hypothesis. It was only through conducting and analyzing many interviews (and really only after about a year of doing so) that I developed a clear idea that my story was about how the Mexican economics profession evolved over time. I changed my research question multiple times, modified my interview guide for almost every participant, and altered the kinds of people I talked to as my topic evolved. Moreover, I had to adapt the location of my interviews to suit the convenience of each participant. I found that retired officials often preferred that I meet them at their homes. One particularly memorable interview, with a former finance minister, took place over lunch at an upscale restaurant in Cuernavaca.

Looking back on it years later, it seemed to me that more recent IRB restrictions would have made my evolving research in Mexico very difficult. According to the letter of the regulations, unforeseen modifications to research design needed to be re-vetted by a board every time before the modified research could commence. Had I been required to file amendments and wait for reapproval each of the dozens of times I incrementally changed my Mexican research, it seems unlikely that I could have completed my study within my year of Fulbright funding.

Another mismatch was the designated role of IRBs in weighing potential risks and benefits. A typical biomedical study often involved risks that were calculable and well-understood—for example, the side effects of venipuncture or tracheal intubation—which were straightforward for boards to assess. But this was seldom the case with a one-of-a-kind study coming from a discipline such as sociology or anthropology.[8] In the absence of good information upon which to estimate risk, IRB decision makers could make subjective and inaccurate assessments.[9] For example, at the time of my research, Mexico was a quasi-dictatorship. Based on this piece of information, an IRB decision maker might have imagined (mistakenly) that I was putting my subjects at risk by having them air their opinions about government policy; an IRB decision maker might have therefore insisted on the standard protection of using pseudonyms in my published results. Because the strength of my findings depended on the attribution of quotes to well-known academics and public officials, this would have greatly impoverished my study.

However, regulatory mismatch was only one dimension of the problem. Just as important were the *interpretations* of local boards; it was local decision makers who were making a regulatory speed bump into a roadblock.[10] During the era of hypercompliance, the culture of a typical research university IRB was one of extreme risk aversion. Widespread confusion about the meaning of federal rules generated a desire for ironclad protection from any conceivable risk of noncompliance, as many of my informants remembered. "The pendulum almost swung too far to the right in terms of the most conservative interpretation of the regulations," recalled Ivy (IRB administrator, independent IRB, retired). This ethos shaped reviewers' decisions, and was institutionalized in formal routines, including standard operating procedures, forms, scripts, and templates. The net effect was to create significant barriers to social and humanities research.

The best known example of hypercompliant interpretation creating such hindrances was IRBs' famous reluctance to allow research to be conducted without signed informed consent documents. These documents were an artifact of a system developed decades earlier to govern biomedical researchers funded by the federal health bureaucracy.[11] According to the regulations, researchers were supposed to acquire signed documents with eight "required elements." These included some items that seemed bizarre in a nonbiomedical setting, such as the "disclosure of appropriate alternative procedures or courses of treatment, if any, that might be advantageous to the subject."

Consent forms, which functioned adequately enough for laboratory research, could pose insurmountable obstacles for ethnographers, who relied on spontaneous encounters in unstructured social settings where the presence of a legal document could appear strange or even threatening.[12] Indeed, the disagreeable legalistic and biomedical language of consent documents posed problems for many qualitative interview-based studies. I feel certain that many of my Mexican informants would have refused to put their signature to such a document.

This latent regulatory mismatch was activated by hypercompliant local interpretations. Although the regulations presented forms as a default, they did not prescribe them universally. In fact, they contained two broad loopholes: boards were allowed to waive either informed consent or the use of signed consent documents (i.e., allowing verbal consent) if the research met certain preconditions. The preconditions for the latter form of waiver could be met by most social and humanities research projects.[13] Yet during the era of hypercompliance, this option fell away, as IRB offices either told investigators that consent forms were mandatory or simply failed to publicize that there was an alternative.[14]

Why were IRBs unwilling to use the leeway that clearly existed within the regulations? There are two particularly compelling explanations. First, flexibility was strongly discouraged by the pervasive uncertainty that prevailed during and immediately following the federal crackdown. Hypercompliance, in informed consent as in other realms, allowed research institutions to buffer themselves against a risky, incalculable environment by creating wide margins that left nothing to chance. Once adopted, hypercompliant practices were contagious, as uncertainly led organizations to imitate their peers.[15]

Second, although the text of the regulations permitted waivers, the underlying logic of the regulations discouraged them. The rules put the burden of proof on investigators to show that they qualified for waivers, and were designed around auditability, exemplified in the motto "If it wasn't documented it didn't happen."[16] Consent documents were not just vehicles for ensuring voluntary participation: they were an integral part of an impeccably compliant auditable record. This imperative, combined with the uncertainty of the crackdown, created a powerful barrier to waiving documentation of consent—to the detriment of researchers in disciplines such as sociology and anthropology.

An Emerging Context for Flexibility

The unhappiness of social researchers with this new regime did not go unnoticed by academic administrators. One of my informants remembered 2005 as "the year of the angry social scientist." Another described social researchers during this period as being like "the townspeople with the pitchforks and torches."

Over time, these sentiments gave rise to a new social movement—one that advocated the use of regulatory flexibility. The flexibility movement was enabled by new circumstances that decreased the appeal of knee-jerk hypercompliance. Most important was the thawing of the regulatory climate. As time passed, there was no renewed outbreak of deadly research scandals such as those that had triggered federal actions in the 1990s. This suggested that the system for protecting human subjects was working, and allowed the attention of lawmakers and regulators to wander to other, more pressing issues. The change in climate was evident in the steady decline in the number

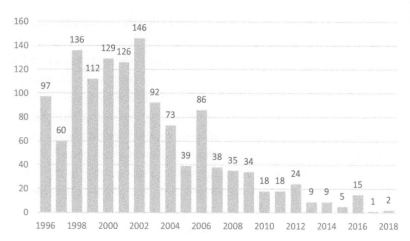

FIGURE 5.1. OPRR/OHRP enforcement letters, 1996–2018. The 2000s figures include both OPRR and OHRP letters of determination. *Sources*: OHRP website; Freedom of Information Act request fulfilled by OHRP.

of enforcement letters issued by the Office for Human Research Protections [OHRP], as illustrated in figure 5.1.[17]

This retreat of federal discipline made institutional decision makers more receptive to arguments for reform. It also mellowed the attitude of IRB professionals, and helped foster the efficiency norms described in chapters 3 and 4. The efficiency ethos provided an amenable bandwagon for the flexibility movement to ride. Although they were inspired by the needs of different researchers, there was a logical affinity between efficiency and flexibility. Spending too much time overregulating minimal-risk research was not only a problem for social researchers; it was a misuse of an IRB office's time and resources. This arguably put participants of truly risky studies at greater peril, as boards wasted time scrutinizing benign research.[18]

Finally, the flexibility movement was enabled by the emergence of influential nonstate actors in the human research protection field. These had been notably absent at the time of the crackdown, when regulators' interactions were often with faculty chairpersons and administrators who had little knowledge of the IRB rules. This—combined with regulatory ambiguity—was conducive to uncertainty and risk-averse hypercompliance.

Since that time, however, the IRB world had become populated by actors who could not only decipher what regulators were saying, but actually talk back. "We were so nervous," Elizabeth recalled of the crackdown years. "We didn't want to make a mistake, and we were like 'oh boy, a lot of risk here.' You see more risk when you lack the knowledge and judgment." Yet as newly minted IRB professionals gained experience and acquired a professional culture, they acquired confidence that enabled a retreat from hypercompliance. As Elizabeth put it, "Now we're much better at saying, 'No, that's not full review, that's expedited. No, that's exempt'" (compliance office director, research university).

The Flexibility Movement

The flexibility movement first emerged among a group of large research universities, where the voices of disgruntled social scientists were amplified by their millions of dollars in sponsored grants. Famous for its Institute for Social Research, the University of Michigan was a congenial incubator for this new initiative. It began with a group of research administrators who were searching for ways to lighten the IRB burden on social and humanities studies.[19] Their initial efforts were focused on unfunded research. For practical reasons, Michigan had decided earlier to "uncheck the box" on its federal-wide assurance. This meant that non–federally funded studies were not covered by all the provisions of the Common Rule, making them abundantly safe to tinker with.

To allay lingering fears of noncompliance, Michigan launched its experiment in 2007 only after consulting with federal regulators and accreditors, and confined it to two innocuous innovations. First, non–federally funded, minimal-risk studies had their continuing review extended to two years (rather than annually). Second, more of these studies were made eligible for exemption, through the development of new exemption categories. Throughout this process, the university remained committed to applying the Belmont principles to all research with human subjects, irrespective of funding source.

The next step was to raise the experiment to the national level. Michigan partnered with other Big Ten universities to pilot a program through the Federal Demonstration Partnership, a forum for discussing issues of research sponsorship and regulation. Federal regulators, who attended partnership meetings, indicated that they did not oppose the project. Participating universities extended approval of unfunded research to two years, as Michigan had already done, and also added exemption categories.

These were modest changes. Yet the spectacle of important research universities deviating from the status quo, with no pushback from regulators and no apparent ill effects, inspired a widespread shift away from reactive risk aversion. IRB administrators took notice. Led by the University of Southern California, the Flexibility Coalition was established in 2011. The coalition developed a web-based guide to help institutions implement "flex" policies and a library of innovations; it quickly acquired more than 100 member organizations.[20]

Flexibility thus grew from a local initiative into a national social movement. One of the movement's most visible effects was to help persuade institutions to uncheck the box in their assurances, and thereby remove unfunded research from the purview of the regulations. In fact, many institutions had been moving in this direction already, having realized that unchecking the box lessened their exposure to compliance risk (since it reduced their formal commitments to federal regulators). By 2015 more than one-third of regulated institutions, including 71 percent of institutions certified by the Association for the Accreditation of Human Research Protection Programs [AAHRPP] had unchecked their boxes.[21] Anecdotal evidence suggests that the practice of unchecking became even more widespread in the years that followed.

"When I first saw people unchecking the box," recalled Amanda, "I was, like, 'Whoa, kind of a risk.' But now I'm like, 'Why wouldn't you uncheck the box?'" (IRB administrator, research university). Institutions that unchecked the box continued to review unfunded research and to apply the Belmont ethics universally. However, by rendering these studies outside the scope of federal audits, unchecking the box could avoid some of the regulations' more burdensome bureaucratic requirements.

Emboldened by these successes, the movement began to apply flexibility to federally funded studies. Within the Federal Demonstration Partnership, a group of faculty and academic administrators—including IRB and other compliance administrators—developed an online guide for reducing burden in the IRB process. Among other things, the guide recommended that IRBs make full use of the informed consent waivers—allowed by the regulations, but widely ignored by research institutions.[22] In 2013, to prevent additional requirements from being imposed on exempt research, the partnership began piloting an "exempt wizard"—an electronic smart form that enabled investigators to apply for exemption without the intervention of an IRB decision maker. It was piloted at New York University, Michigan State University, Boston University, and the University of Washington, among other institutions.

Once launched, flexibility innovations diffused rapidly. A particularly important vehicle for this diffusion was the accrediting agency, AAHRPP. The accreditor's reputation for rigor was fearsome, and its seal of approval was respected by federal regulators. Yet, unlike regulators, AAHRPP could provide clear, routinely updated feedback on what practices were possible and desirable within the framework of the regulations. This created greater confidence, and made it possible for local institutions to try new things. For example, AAHRPP was consulted before Michigan launched its first trial initiatives to expand the continuing review period, and before the initiative was expanded to other Big Ten institutions.[23] AAHRPP indicated its support and began to allow and even encourage its own clients to uncheck the box, and to adopt more flexible policies.

The AAHRPP imprimatur legitimated flexibility and inspired IRBs around the country to slough off many hypercompliant policies. As Owen recalled:

> I remember hearing about the experiments that Michigan was engaging in a while back . . . and I remember bringing that to the attention of my boss at the time and the attitude was very much like, "They're taking on too much risk, and they're gonna get shut down" . . . and as it turned out those experiments are now very widely adopted. . . . AAHRPP opened us up to accepting those things, because it was clear that these were best practices. (IRB administrator, research university)

Inspired by these novel best practices, some IRB administrators began to serve as local advocates for flexibility. Several of my respondents recalled persuading risk-averse upper administrators that flexibility innovations, such as unchecking the box or creating new exemption categories, were safe.

Both accreditors and the IRB profession also provided lines of communication across which the flexibility gospel could spread. PRIM&R meetings supplied a particularly important forum for diffusing flexibility to rank-and-file practitioners. In 2007, the organization's social and behavioral conference introduced a special track on "Finding Flexibility within the Regulations." One panel was revealingly titled "What Do *Your* Investigators Complain about Most? Come and Explore Ethical Ways to Find Flexibility while Being Compliant." Another panel featured federal regulators presenting on flexibility.[24] In the years that followed, flexibility-themed panels became PRIM&R conference staples, and were listed as suitable for attendees preparing for the Certified IRB Professional examination.[25]

The consequences of the movement's efforts were palpable. Many of my informants reported that there had been a widespread shift "away from a risk-averse position . . . driven by fear of being shut down . . . more toward a reinterpretation of the guidelines to allow more flexibility," as Griffin explained (IRB faculty chairperson, research university). A majority of my informants reported having adopted one or more innovations associated with the flexibility movement. For example, Lara reported that her institution actively encouraged social researchers to avoid consent documentation: "We tell [social researchers], as much as possible, to not get a signature" (IRB administrator, research university).

These innovations were certainly not universal. My sample of informants was biased toward individuals who could be described as "thought leaders" in the field, rather than everyday practitioners. Some boards were undoubtedly more insulated than others from emerging best practices, and some IRB administrators were constitutionally inclined toward the older ways. For example, William exemplified the earlier ethos. "The culture that I have cultivated in this position is to always err on the side of caution," he explained. "Just to be as conservative as we can when it comes to protecting human subjects" (IRB administrator, liberal arts college).

Moreover, even among IRB professionals who agreed with flexibility in principle, there were varying degrees of endorsement. Some practices, such as longer continuing review periods for unfunded research, inspired widespread support. Others were more controversial. One more contentious innovation was the Federal Demonstration Partnership's electronic exempt decision tool—an online algorithm to be used by investigators to determine whether or not their research was exempt. An implicit rationale for the tool was that staff reviewers were known to use the exemption process to introduce additional requirements—such as informed consent documents with standard regulatory language—that robbed exemption of its original meaning. Although the tool was supported by many flexibility advocates, in 2015 PRIM&R objected to including it in revisions to the Common Rule.[26] Their objection was founded on the seminal principle of the IRB system: namely, that researchers had too great a conflict of interest to be trusted to make decisions about their own studies.

Yet even if they were embraced unevenly, the norms of flexibility were important. The movement had changed the taken-for-granted assumptions of the field and shifted the spectrum of thinkable thought about what constituted acceptable research behavior.

The Feds Get on Board

The workaround state encourages nongovernmental actors to define what it means to comply. These actors clarify complex and ambiguous rules by establishing industry standards—best practices that the state subsequently endorses.[27] This dynamic was clearly evident in the flexibility movement. Pioneered by academic administrators, bolstered by accreditors, and diffused by IRB professionals, the norms of flexibility were at first tolerated by federal agencies. Later, their support became explicit, when long-overdue revisions to federal regulations contained elements long championed by flexibility advocates. In subtle but significant ways, the flexibility movement had succeeded in redefining compliance.

The revised Common Rule, which took full effect in January 2019, was the culmination of a multiyear quest "to better protect human subjects . . . while facilitating valuable research and reducing burden, delay, and ambiguity for investigators."[28] Although the rule's leading focus was on the biomedical field, it also referenced the particular issues of social and humanities researchers. Released in the summer of 2011, the rule's Advanced Notice of Proposed Rulemaking acknowledged that "questions have been raised about the appropriateness of the review process for social and behavioral research," and cited numerous reports and academic studies to this point.[29]

Social and humanities researchers fervently hoped for a final rule that would conclusively address these concerns. The results were perhaps less conclusive than we would have liked. The biggest winners were oral historians and journalists whose investigations were, for the first time, officially deemed not to be "research," and hence outside the scope of the regulations.[30] On the other hand, the final rule omitted a number of suggestions, considered earlier in the rulemaking process, that might have been beneficial to researchers in disciplines such as sociology. These discarded options included an ambitious proposal to "excuse" most social and humanities research from IRB review; an explicit exemption category for participant observation, something for which anthropologists had long fought; a requirement that IRBs have an appeals mechanism; and a federally designed electronic exemption tool.[31]

Nevertheless, for the flexibility movement the new rule represented a significant achievement. It entirely eliminated continuing review of minimal risk research, an extension of a best practice the movement had pioneered. Also in line with flexibility innovations, the rule contained new exemption categories, including one for "benign behavioral interventions," expected to benefit many researchers in psychology. And although the exemption tool did not make it into the final Common Rule, in the preamble, regulators indicated their ongoing support for the idea: "We continue to believe that a well-designed, tested, and validated exemption decision tool could offer an expedient mechanism for determining whether research studies are exempt. Thus, we will continue to explore development of an exemption decision tool."[32] This left open the possibility that regulators might in the future develop such a tool—or that they might endorse institutions' developing electronic tools of their own.[33] Indeed, as this book neared completion, it appeared that the University of Michigan was piloting an exemption decision tool within its protocol management system.

Most strikingly, the preamble announced a significant change to regulatory procedures: institutions would no longer have the option of pledging to apply the Common Rule to unfunded research. For years, institutions filing assurances with OHRP had the option to either check or uncheck the box on their assurance forms; but now, the box would be removed, thereby eliminating a significant incubator of hypercompliance. As the preamble explained:

> We expect this change to have the beneficial effect of encouraging some institutions to explore a variety of flexible approaches to overseeing low risk research that is not funded by a Common Rule department or agency, without reducing protection of human subjects, thus furthering the goal to decrease inappropriate administrative burdens.[34]

In addition to this idealistic reasoning, the agency likely had a more practical motive: with a staff that had dwindled significantly since the crackdown years, OHRP clearly lacked the resources to oversee all human subjects studies at every federally funded institution in the country.

Of all the changes accompanying the publication of the new rule, eliminating the box on the assurance form seemed to have the greatest potential benefit for social research, most of which was not funded by federal agencies. As two social scientists noted in the *Chronicle of Higher Education* in 2017, "OHRP has made it clear that it has no interest in overseeing research not funded by agencies bound by the Common Rule . . . [and] given its blessing to those who wish to experiment in new ways of managing low-risk research that is not federally funded. This is welcome guidance—now it is time for us to move forward with reform."[35]

As this book goes to press, readers from social and humanities disciplines continue to wonder what the new Common Rule will mean for us. It is important to remember that how we fared under the old regulations was variable and always depended on how institutions and IRBs chose to interpret them.

These interpretations, in turn, were informed by institutions' varying perceptions of federal threat. And it seems improbable that there will ever be a sequel to the state of high anxiety that launched the era of hypercompliance. Someday, there will undoubtedly be a fresh outbreak of research scandals, and the regulatory pendulum will swing back to a more disciplinary position. But today the vast majority of clinical trials are privately sponsored and regulated by FDA, rather than federally funded and regulated by OHRP.[36] Consequently, research misdeeds will likely be handled by an agency that penalizes individual investigators and boards more than it does research institutions. This suggests that a future crackdown will be less likely to cause a hypercompliant reaction among universities, and hence less likely to affect social and humanities researchers.

Although these are all promising signs, the fact is that whether and how much flexibility is put into practice remains in the hands of local authorities: in our highly decentralized ethics review system, they are free to adhere to the most conservative reading of the regulations if they choose to do so. It will fall to social and humanities researchers to remind local authorities that unfunded studies are no longer subject to the Common Rule, that exempt means exempt, and that consent forms can make a qualitative project less feasible without making it more ethical.

6

Varieties of Compliance

"THOSE WHO ARE EQUAL BEFORE GOD shall now also be equal in the polling booths, in the classrooms, in the factories, and in hotels, restaurants, movie theaters, and other places that provide service to the public."[1] With these words, President Lyndon B. Johnson signed into law the Civil Rights Act of 1964, which would fundamentally reshape American organizations in both intended and unintended ways.

One entirely unforeseen consequence was compliance bureaucracy. The Civil Rights Act neither defined discrimination nor created an agency with the authority to set official precedents. In the area of employment discrimination, the potency of the law lay not in its federal enforcement apparatus—the resources and authority of which were meager—but rather in its embedded "private right of action," which allowed employers to be sued for alleged discrimination. What this meant in practice was that the meaning of civil rights law would be defined by a large and growing number of court cases. Because these judicial interpretations varied across judges and over time, the meaning of compliance was ambiguous and unstable. Organizations responded to such uncertainty by investing in equal employment opportunity (EEO) offices within personnel departments, where staff tracked the changing meaning of employment law and administered local policies to keep their employers from being sued. Over time, these workers grew into a national profession that set standards, or "best practices," that came to define the meaning of compliance.

The story of these unintended consequences of the Civil Rights Act has been told many times, and most of what we know about compliance bureaucracy is derived from this case.[2] Yet EEO is only the best known of a much larger array of compliance fields: variants on the compliance species can be found in universities, hospitals, and private firms across the United States, covering a host of regulatory areas, ranging from human subjects protections to financial services, health care privacy, and occupational safety and health—and undoubtedly many others that have not yet attracted scholarly attention.[3]

This book has explored the case of IRB administration and shown it to be both similar and dissimilar to EEO offices. One of the most striking differences has to do with efficiency orientation. We have seen that over time, the practices of IRB offices, especially in the biomedical field, became increasingly oriented toward accomplishing more work in less time, using fewer resources, and intruding less on core activities. The most visible hallmarks of this approach included the extensive use of rationalizing tools, such as automating IRB software, and the outsourcing of reviews to for-profit, independent boards that could process them more conveniently.

In contrast, the extensive scholarship on EEO administration has not observed the widespread adoption of efficiency-enhancing best practices. Rather, authors who study EEO offices have more often described them as embracing *symbolic* best practices, designed not to improve speed and reduce costs, but to signal to powerful outsiders (especially judges in lawsuits) that organizations are "doing [their] best to figure out how to comply."[4] In short, studies of EEO paint a portrait of compliance bureaucracy that is notably different from what we have seen in the earlier chapters in this book.

How can we account for this contrast between efficiency-embracing biomedical IRBs, on the one hand, and good faith-performing EEO offices, on the other? In this chapter I address this question through a comparison among IRB, EEO, and financial services compliance fields. I argue that both the IRB and financial services fields were dominated by a logic of auditability, an overriding imperative to follow and document adherence to formally defined procedures. This made compliance quite expensive for regulated organizations and led to the adoption of cost-controlling best practices, such as automating software and outsourcing to external compliance firms. Contrastingly, EEO offices were not primarily organized around auditability, and therefore were not pressured to innovate in this way. These differences suggest two distinct varieties of compliance: symbolic compliance, assessed in court cases that reward recognizable gestures of good faith; and auditable compliance, assessed in regulatory investigations that place a premium on following predefined procedures and keeping meticulous records.

The Embrace of Efficiency in Financial Services Compliance

"It's been about a year since the meltdown at Enron Corp. began in earnest, and what a year it has been," reported the magazine *Financial Executive*. "The drumbeat of negative headlines has been almost incessant, and the corporate miscreants and their misdeeds are so well known that few financial managers need a recap."[5] The year was 2002, and corporate accounting scandals were resulting in billions of dollars in federal penalties and damages, along with prison sentences for some offending executives. President George W. Bush signed into law the Sarbanes-Oxley Act, designed to improve corporate financial disclosure and prevent accounting fraud. Corporate executives scrambled to respond to extensive new regulatory requirements, often by making significant investments in compliance offices.[6]

A sequel occurred a half-decade later, with the outbreak of the financial crisis—followed by another wave of federal enforcement and the passage of the Dodd-Frank Act, which placed extensive new regulations on financial firms.[7] These events shook the finance industry to its core and generated even greater investments in compliance administration. For example, at JP Morgan, there were reportedly around 8,000 compliance and control personnel hired following the passage of Dodd-Frank.[8] There was a steady rise in salaries and a bidding war among firms seeking to recruit qualified compliance staff.[9]

The purpose of compliance bureaucracy in financial services, just as in the EEO and IRB fields, was to protect organizations against misalignment with government rules. In the financial industry, where clients typically signed mandatory arbitration clauses, the leading risk was not private litigation but rather federal penalties. These included not only fines—JP Morgan alone paid out billions of dollars for its role in the financial crisis—but also criminal prosecution, jail time, and lasting reputational damage.

To address these risks, a new group of skilled workers emerged and acquired a professional identity. They subscribed to the same trade publications and became members of the National Society of Compliance Professionals, "dedicated to serving and supporting the compliance professional in the financial services industry."[10] And they developed best practices that were oriented toward accomplishing compliance labor more efficiently, exemplified in two popular innovations: the universal adoption of sophisticated, labor-saving electronic tools; and the outsourcing of compliance work to specialized external compliance bureaucracies.

Adherence to the financial services rules was very labor-intensive—more so than it was with the EEO or even the IRB regulations. The reason was the greater complexity and scope of the financial services regulations and their intended object. The activities being overseen were vast, complex, rapid, and constantly evolving. Firms were required to monitor not only thousands of daily transactions, but also employee telephone and e-mail communications. There were detailed rules for how to investigate suspicious activities and how to format and file reports on these activities with regulators. And there were strict requirements for exhaustive reporting to regulators, as well as the storage of astronomical quantities of data, to be used in case of a regulatory audit, and for which top management could be held personally responsible.[11]

These rules were spectacularly fragmented, overlapping, and overseen by multiple agencies such as the Securities and Exchange Commission (SEC), the Commodity Futures Trading Commission (CFTC), the Office of the Comptroller of the Treasury, the Federal Reserve, the Department of Labor (for worker pensions), and the Federal Deposit Insurance Corporation. It also included an array of nongovernmental regulators, including the National Futures Association (NFA), the Municipal Securities Rulemaking Board (MSRB), and the Financial Institution National Regulatory Association (FINRA). There were also the rules of state-level agencies and—as firms expanded their global operations—other national regulatory systems.[12]

With so many regulators in the mix, staff needed to track and respond to ongoing changes in the rules—changes that could number in the hundreds every month.[13]

To tackle this mountain of exacting work, compliance offices made growing use of electronic tools to manage many different dimensions of the job. For example, "rule management" software could automatically adapt firm practices to changing regulations and guidance, while other electronic tools could be used to monitor employee communications or to store data in a format that could be easily retrieved for auditors and regular reports. So ubiquitous was this software that it acquired a popular moniker: "regtech," short for "regulatory technology."

Regtech was not cheap. An electronic transaction monitoring system alone could cost upwards of $50,000 a year—and this was only one of the many types of electronic tools that a firm might need to purchase.[14] The largest firms invested great sums in developing and maintaining their own customized, in-house electronic systems. Its high price tag notwithstanding, regtech was widely adopted because it was viewed as indispensable. It kept track of a vast array of rigorous regulatory details and prevented workers from engaging in noncompliant activities when communicating online. Regtech also kept compliance from interfering unduly with the revenue-generating work of bankers. "Regulatory compliance is a cost of doing business," explained a bank's chief compliance officer in a 2003 interview. "Our goal is to implement efficient processes and procedures that will relieve the regulatory burden from our frontline bankers. We are constantly evaluating our processes for additional automation opportunities."[15]

Just as importantly, regtech was designed to control the prodigious expense of maintaining compliance staff, who could number in the thousands at the larger firms. Under pressure from hard budget constraints, compliance offices sought to automate more functions.[16] For example, according to one financial reporter in 2017, technology could even help with the skilled labor of regulatory interpretation:

> At the moment every new rule has to be read and interpreted by a human being, which is time-consuming and prone to errors. NLP [Natural Language

Processing software] can help identify the requirements that are contained within a document and, using the entities and metadata, determine to whom they apply and to what products, topics and processes they relate. On an ongoing basis, machines can then continue to monitor compliance.[17]

The routinization and automation of financial services compliance was reminiscent of the IRB field, where there was extensive use of protocol management software—the IRB version of regtech. However, in financial services electronic tools were used far more extensively, fueled by government requirements that were considerably more confusing and demanding.

A second hallmark of the efficiency orientation was outsourcing. According to a 2017 survey of the financial services field, 28 percent of firms were partially or completely engaging the services of "compliance management" firms.[18] Regulators warned that offloading compliance in this way might cause top leadership to lose sight of their legal and ethical commitments.[19] However, these warnings did not prevent the practice from steadily increasing in popularity. Outsourcing was particularly important for smaller companies that could not afford a large team of full-time compliance administrators. Even a relatively well-staffed compliance office might choose to outsource specific functions for which it lacked expertise.[20]

Here, too, there were obvious parallels to human research protections, where outsourcing to independent IRBs became a common practice. In both cases, managing compliance was labor-intensive; sometimes it was more efficient to pay a vendor to get the job done. And in both fields, independent vendors competed for clients in a compliance marketplace, encouraging the spread of efficiency norms and an ethos of customer service.

Accounting for the Difference

Whether they manage equal employment opportunity, human research protections, or rules for financial transactions, different varieties of compliance bureaucracy share common family traits. One example is the workplace training program, which seems to be a universal marker of the compliance genus. Whereas equal opportunity offices became famous for their diversity training workshops, IRB professionals participated in the creation of the CITI

TABLE 6.1

*Frequency of Monthly Trade Journal
Articles Using the Terms "Efficient," "Efficiently," or
"Efficiency," 2009–2018*

EEO	
Insight into Diversity	4
Profiles in Diversity	17
Human research protections	
IRB Advisor	203
Financial services/corporate governance risk	
Compliance Week[a]	679

SOURCES: Nexis Uni (*IRB Advisor*), Academic OneFile (*Compliance Week*), and EBSCO (*Insight into Diversity* and *Profiles in Diversity*).
[a]Despite its misleading name, *Compliance Week* is a monthly publication.

(Collaborative Institutional Training Initiative) online researcher education program. In financial services, compliance staff similarly required frontline workers to take online modules purchased from vendors of "learning management systems."

Yet compliance fields also vary. The financial services and IRB fields were characterized by efficiency-enhancing best practices—regtech and outsourcing—that were notably absent in EEO, a contrast reflected in the rhetoric of the different fields. Table 6.1 depicts variations in the frequency of the use of the terms "efficient," "efficiently," or "efficiency" in monthly trade journals catering to the three compliance professions. It shows that whereas these terms were pervasive in the IRB and financial services publications, they were practically nonexistent in the two EEO journals.

These rhetorical patterns reinforce the idea that in IRB and financial services, compliance was treated more as a technical problem than it was in EEO. In the remainder of this chapter I argue that technical pressures arise in fields where compliance offices are defined by a *logic of auditability*[21]—that is to say, where they are required to mass-produce tangible, precise indicators of compliance designed to be exhaustively scrutinized by regulatory authorities. The auditability imperative makes compliance intrusive and expensive, giving rise to best practices designed to improve efficiency. In contrast, EEO offices were defined by what some organizational sociologists term a "logic of confidence"—they were designed to signal an organization's good faith, which subjected them to weaker efficiency pressures.[22]

Two Logics of Compliance

Compliance bureaucracies occupy a liminal space between the state and regulated organizations: they exert tremendous influence on how compliance is defined, but they do not have the final say. State authorities are the ultimate arbiters of what compliance entails but they exercise this power in very different ways, depending on the nature of the compliance regime. The EEO system was at one time characterized by two different varieties of enforcement: federal compliance reviews, on the one hand, and discrimination lawsuits, enabled by the Civil Rights Act's private right of action, on the other. But with the deregulation of the 1980s federal reviews dwindled, and it fell to judges in lawsuits to define the boundaries of compliance.[23] Judges in workplace discrimination cases were famous for assessing whether organizations could present visible indicators of good faith, such as diversity training programs and offices dedicated to diversity promotion.[24]

In contrast, the dominant arbiters of compliance in the IRB and financial services fields were always regulatory offices that engaged in audits: formal investigations assessing adherence to rules that, while ambiguous in many respects, were explicit in many others. Audits have a central role in systems of enforced self-regulation, which delegate oversight to local compliance offices. Rather than governing organizations directly, regulators focus on overseeing compliance offices, themselves charged with overseeing their respective organizations—a nested system Michael Power describes as the "control of control."[25] In the cases of IRB and financial services, there was also an extra layer of intermediaries—nongovernmental organizations that set additional rules and standards for compliance offices to follow, and that also conducted audits. Standards for IRBs were set by AAHRPP (the Association for the Accreditation of Human Protection Programs); in financial services, they were established by nongovernmental regulators such as FINRA. The structure of enforced self-regulation in the two regimes is depicted in figure 6.1.

In both frameworks, compliance offices drafted their own policies to be consistent with the policy goals of regulators and intermediaries, and applied

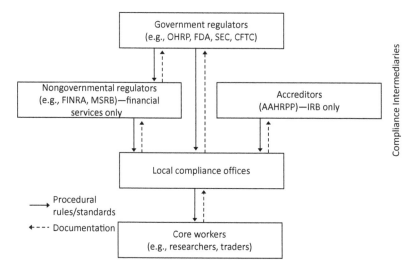

FIGURE 6.1. Enforced self-regulation in IRB and financial services.

them to front-line workers and others in the organization. Regulators and intermediaries were empowered to conduct audits to ensure that compliance offices were upholding federal rules, intermediaries' standards, and their own local policies. To facilitate this oversight, IRB and financial services compliance offices were required to create and maintain extensive auditable records demonstrating that rules had been followed. Since both systems emphasized procedures rather than measurable outcomes, it was absolutely essential to produce written records to document that compliance had occurred. The IRB field's mantra, "If it wasn't documented, it didn't happen," was echoed in financial services: "If it's not in writing, it's as if [it] did not occur."[26]

This logic of auditability had two key implications. First, organizations had to adhere closely to the letter of the rules, because deviations from auditable standards could be detected and sanctioned. Second, auditability entailed high costs for regulated organizations.[27] It could intrude significantly on core work activities, to the extent that it required core workers to participate in the production of auditable indicators. For example, before launching a biomedical study, a researcher might need to complete a long form framed in confusing regulatory language, and resubmit it multiple times to ensure that mandated decision criteria were considered and duly documented. Front-line bankers might similarly get ensnarled in paperwork designed to document adherence to federal mandates.[28] This could not only aggravate workers, but also divert their valuable time from the core work of the organization.

The logic of auditability also made compliance quite expensive. As delegated authorities, compliance offices were charged with making, updating, and applying a host of formal rules to organizations and their workers—and with generating, organizing, and storing reams of documentation to show that these rules had been applied and followed. The magnitude of this job was compounded by the chaotic structure of the workaround state, as was especially evident in financial services, where compliance offices had to navigate the requirements of a veritable alphabet soup of regulatory agencies and intermediaries. All this was a lot of work—and it was the sort of work that could not be entrusted to secretaries at the bottom of the pay scale. In financial services, compliance reportedly cost the industry $270 billion in 2017, or about 10 percent of total operating resources.[29]

The high price of auditable compliance confronted both the IRB and financial services fields with technical problems: how to follow the rules in less time, using fewer resources, and with less disruption to core activities. This led them to common solutions: the rationalization of compliance work through routines and electronic automation; and the outsourcing of compliance services to specialized firms that could provide them either more quickly or more cost-effectively.

Contrastingly, compliance with antidiscrimination law was less expensive and less disruptive to the core work of the organization. A judge in a discrimination lawsuit was not scouring comprehensive written records to assess whether detailed rules had been followed each and every time, but was rather broadly assessing an organization's "visible commitment to law."[30] Because demonstrating good faith was comparatively less expensive for organizations, it created fewer incentives for innovation.

This comparison suggests an analytical distinction between two different varieties of compliance, illustrated in table 6.2. Symbolic compliance, as exemplified by EEO, is enforced through lawsuits and assessed by courts. Auditable

TABLE 6.2

Symbolic and Auditable Compliance Regimes Compared

	Symbolic Compliance (EEO)	Auditable Compliance (IRB, financial services)
Enforcement mechanism	Lawsuits	Audits
Assessors of compliance	Courts	Regulatory bureaucracies: —Governmental (e.g., OHRP, SEC) —Nongovernmental (e.g., FINRA)
Compliance indicators	Evidence of good faith	Reports and auditable documentation
Efficiency orientation	Low	High

compliance is enforced in formal investigations conducted by bureaucratic agencies. Whereas in the former, organizations indicate compliance by providing evidence of good faith, in the latter, they generate large volumes of documentation to demonstrate that specific procedures have been followed, creating high costs and efficiency pressures.

Intriguingly, this pattern appears to be borne out in recent dynamics around Title IX of the Education Amendments of 1972, which prohibits sex discrimination in federally funded education.[31] Like EEO compliance, the boundaries of Title IX were historically defined by lawsuits; in theory, regulators could sanction noncompliant institutions by suspending federal funding, but in practice this lever was never used.[32] As a result, Title IX had the characteristics of a symbolic regime; compliance was mostly assessed by courts, and local administrative expenses were relatively low.

During the Obama administration, however, Title IX was suddenly pulled into closer alignment with the more specific demands of federal regulators. The agency in charge of overseeing Title IX—the Office of Civil Rights in the Department of Education—initiated a campaign to combat sexual harassment and sexual assault on college campuses. It launched a series of reputation-damaging campus investigations, and published extensive guidance. Universities were required to provide not only training, but also (among other things) to promptly investigate all complaints, usually within sixty days. They were also required to implement annual questionnaires to assess the climate around sexual violence and gender roles. Every federal investigation was accompanied by an extensive review of a school's policies and records of student conduct and complaints; institutions were often admonished for insufficient recordkeeping.[33]

In this way, Title IX began to acquire more of the characteristics of an auditable compliance regime. The increased demand for documented procedures made compliance considerably more disruptive and labor-intensive. In response, universities began to use specialized software to track and store records related to student conduct, public safety incidents, and institutional responses to sexual misconduct. One such software package, Maxient, received a nod from *University Business* in 2014 as a "reader's top choice" product.[34] Strikingly, because federal guidance required very short timelines for completion of disciplinary proceedings, universities also began to hire outside investigators to get the job done.[35] Thus, like IRB and financial services compliance, the Title IX world exhibited an apparent movement toward efficiency innovations, as evidenced by the use of specialized software and outsourcing.

Of course, this move toward auditability was modest compared to analogous trends in IRB and financial services, and it was rolled back by the Trump administration shortly thereafter. Nevertheless, the case of Title IX provides further evidence that introducing demands for auditable, predefined compliance outputs creates technical demands for efficiency.

The Consequences of Compliance Regimes

Compliance bureaucracy is a genus containing more than one species. We have seen that unlike compliance fields defined by a logic of confidence, those structured by a logic of auditability must confront ongoing technical problems. Faced with the high cost of following the letter of the rules, compliance offices continuously strive to make the process more unobtrusive and economical.

This pursuit of efficiency does not necessarily imply that auditable systems are effective at pursuing social goals. The rationalizing tools of bureaucracy are very often deployed to serve less than rational ends, and the logic of the audit may create incentives for elaborate "games of compliance."[36] For example, some critics of the IRB system have charged that it encourages a ritualistic focus on following and documenting review procedures rather than upholding ethical principles.[37]

Yet whether or not they are entirely effective, auditable compliance regimes are almost certainly more consequential than symbolic regimes for the organizations in their orbit. Auditable systems are designed to penetrate deep into core activities and to fundamentally alter organizational routines.[38] This places them at the convergence of two potent countervailing pressures—the external demand for compliance on the one hand and the internal demand for cost control on the other. Technical innovations designed to improve efficiency ameliorate this tension but do not resolve it. Rather, the compliance-efficiency balance in auditable regimes is variable and in constant flux, depending on the shifting regulatory environment.

Moreover, because they significantly enlarge and intrude on organizations' daily labors, it is auditable compliance systems that provide more fertile ground for the flourishing of for-profit compliance service firms. While symbolic compliance may give rise to private consultants and employee training programs, these are dwarfed by the satellite industries that proliferate under auditable regimes, where organizations are willing pay large sums to control the high expense of following the rules.

Conclusion

ON JANUARY 19, 2017, only one day before the inauguration of President Donald J. Trump, federal authorities published a revised Common Rule. It was the culmination of an arduous journey, spanning more than five years, two public notices, and multiple delays.

Like the old rules, the new rules were complex, ambiguous, and difficult to summarize. For biomedical researchers, one major highlight was the requirement of single IRB review for federally funded studies conducted across multiple sites. The new regulations also addressed the controversial use of biospecimens (such as blood, urine, or cells) in new research projects for which they had not been originally collected: researchers would need to obtain "broad consent" to use subjects' identifiable specimens in future studies, with no consent required for specimens that could not be identified.[1] For social, behavioral, and humanities researchers, the new regulations brought an assortment of blessings (described in chapter 5) consistent with a more flexible approach.

Yet perhaps the most notable feature of the new Common Rule was its continuity with the old. "All they did was tinker around the edges," complained Claire. "You would think if they took that much time we could have something like a Belmont Report 2.0" (research administrator, research university). The essential framework was left intact, and—although the new rule applied to research sponsored by twenty different agencies—commercial studies would continue to be governed by a different, albeit similar, set of regulations overseen by the U.S. Food and Drug Administration (FDA).

Meanwhile, the regulations would continue to be confusing and inaccessible to non-IRB experts. In some ways they became more confusing. For example, some exempt research was now required to go through "limited IRB review"—an oxymoron, since exempt research was, by definition, not supposed to be reviewed, and an added source of complication to exemption determinations. The FDA regulations were not updated in tandem with the new Common Rule, which meant that the gap between them was wider than ever, at least temporarily. As this book went to press in 2019, harmonized FDA regulations were planned but still pending.[2]

For their part, regulators would continue to provide noncommittal non-clarifications of what it meant to comply. On the eve of the rollout of most of its provisions, the new Common Rule still had many gray areas. "There have been scattering bits of guidance, but there are big chunks of it we don't have guidance on," explained one research administrator.[3] IRB professionals would have a central role in interpreting the new regulations, just as they had in the old.

From Compliance Bureaucracy to Compliance Marketplace

This book has told the story of an earlier transformation: the evolution of IRBs from collegial bodies into compliance bureaucracies. This shift was triggered not by new regulations, but by the harsh regulatory climate of the federal crackdown. To insulate themselves from the risk of government sanctions, research institutions placed compliance in the hands of paid staff. Their role was not only to decipher and define ambiguous federal rules, but also to ensure that their employers had impeccable records of procedural compliance, to be produced in the event of a federal audit. Later, compliance professionals took charge of making sure that meticulous rule-following would pose minimal obstruction to the research enterprise. For their part, faculty volunteers were happy enough to leave these exacting, time-consuming duties to the professionals.

The tale of the rise of compliance bureaucracy in IRBs is one that illuminates deeper features of American governance. Throughout the system's evolution, a constant has been what I have called the workaround state: a pattern in American politics and institutions marked by the emergence of ingenious, private alternatives to would-be government functions.[4] Sometimes workarounds are devised deliberately by policy makers seeking to circumvent limited state capacity. In other instances, they emerge as an organic, unintended adaptation. In either case, private actors, associations, and organizations become powerful co-participants in governance.

Compliance bureaucracy in human research protections, in alliance with its close cousin, compliance accreditation, is a revealing example. It emerged as both an intended and unintended consequence of a federal system that lacked a strong, centralized body to make system-wide decisions and set ethical precedents. Regulators with limited resources and authority engaged in variable, inconsistent clarification and enforcement. When they did begin to enforce on a large scale, during the federal crackdown, it was to sanction not ethical breaches but procedural failures. These shortcomings generated systemic problems, including inconsistent IRB decisions, reactive hypercompliance, and costly proceduralism.[5]

Into this primordial chaos, compliance bureaucracy stepped to provide rationalizing structure. Whereas the federal system may have remained messy and confusing, at the institutional level things became more orderly and predictable. This was thanks partly to the work of local compliance administrators and the profession that knit these disparate workers into a connected national whole. It also owed much to the Association for the Accreditation of Human Protection Programs (AAHRPP), which compensated for the absence of sustained federal oversight and comprehensive guidance by setting standards and engaging in regular site visits.

Over time, this world began to acquire the characteristics of a private industry governed by market forces. Industrialization was driven by a powerful imperative to render scrupulous compliance less costly for the biomedical research enterprise. Independent IRBs—stand-alone, for-profit compliance bureaucracies—were at the vanguard of this trend. Adapted to the fast-paced field of commercial biomedicine, they were famously more efficient than their traditional IRB counterparts. Where local boards arrived at disparate decisions that had to be laboriously reconciled, independent boards offered rapid single review of even the most arcane, geographically dispersed proposals. By 2016, they were handling nearly three-quarters of clinical trials in in the United States.[6]

With the rollout of the new Common Rule, the role of independent boards seemed certain to increase even more. The rule's single IRB requirement was the culmination of a long-term shift in the regulatory climate—a turning of federal attention away from ethical abuses, and toward removing needless encumbrances to lifesaving research. In 2010, single IRB review began to be encouraged for federally sponsored research by the Office of Human Research Protections (OHRP).[7] In 2016, the National Institutes of Health (NIH) began to require single IRB review of the multisite research it funded, and to permit investigators to charge IRB fees as direct costs to their grants.[8] At the end of that same year, President Barack Obama signed into law the 21st Century Cures Act, which, among many other things, removed restrictions on the use of single IRBs in medical device trials.[9] The largest independent board, WIRB-Copernicus, had lobbied on behalf of this legislation.[10]

Washington's embrace of single IRB review was widely seen as a boon to the commercial IRB industry. There were noncommercial options: some government institutions had their own single IRBs, and some larger traditional boards were adapting by becoming the "IRB of record" in multisite studies.[11] However, these would face stiff competition from independent boards with decades of experience with single IRB review, along with cutting-edge software, crack legal teams, and extensive networks of reviewers for hire. The comparative advantage of independent boards would be further enhanced by changes to NIH rules permitting the payment of IRB fees as direct costs on grants. What this meant, in effect, was that grant recipients could exercise consumer choice in a marketplace of review services—and that a growing number might choose independent over traditional IRBs.[12]

This widening of the independent IRBs' customer base had at least three major implications. First, traditional boards would likely lose staff positions (as a number of my respondents reported) due to the loss of reviews to independent boards. This would have little impact on the small offices reviewing social and humanities research, most of which was not funded and not a market for independent IRB services. Its greatest impact would be on biomedical

IRBs with large amounts of sponsored research overseen by large compliance staffs. After decades of impressive growth, membership in PRIM&R (Public Responsibility in Medicine and Research) began to decline slightly.[13]

Second, there would be even more pressure on traditional boards to emulate the practices of their independent brethren. An example could be found in the case of a university that eliminated the overhead budget for its IRB office, allowing it to run entirely on fees charged to private and public sponsors.[14] Although this response was unusually radical, it illustrated the cold winds of competition to which traditional IRBs would need to adapt. Even if for-profit IRBs did not take over the system, their ethos of efficiency and client services would become ever more influential.

Third, although the IRB profession faced little danger of going extinct, it would surely evolve. It seemed poised to become a smaller profession, as armies of checklist-wielding staff at academic medical centers were replaced by smaller, more elite cadres using cutting-edge compliance software, and more often working at independent boards. It would depend less on the good-will of academic administrators, and more on the decisions of individual investigators, sponsors, and subcontractors who exercised choice in the marketplace of compliance services. The profession would survive by adapting.

The American Model in Comparative Perspective

The American model for protecting human research subjects is not the only possible model. Around the world, wealthy democracies have developed a range of different mechanisms for this purpose, all of which entrust ethical judgments to qualified committees. These deliberative bodies are embedded in different policy frameworks, reflecting varying national cultures, histories, and institutions. On one end of the spectrum is a group of nations with highly decentralized systems, including not only the United States, but also Canada and Australia.[15] On the other end of the spectrum are many European countries, where committees are more closely coordinated by government ministries.[16]

The United Kingdom is a particularly interesting case: once strongly resembling its American counterpart, the British system recently moved toward European-style centralization. As late as the 1990s, the United Kingdom had more than 200 local boards, loosely supervised by health authorities. With an increasingly unmanageable workload, and with multisite research on the rise, the British system was prone to problems very similar to those being discussed across the Atlantic. There was "a groundswell of complaint from research workers, frustrated at the delays incurred, the costs involved, and the unnecessary duplication of effort," leading to a call for a fundamental reorganization.[17]

However, whereas parallel calls for policy change in the United States were thwarted by insurmountable obstacles (see chapter 1), the British government was able to initiate major reforms. The Department of Health began to standardize the system, and inaugurated a structure of region-based committees to serve as lead boards in multisite clinical trials.[18] In 2000 it established a national Central Office for Research Ethics Committees, which implemented mechanisms to improve boards' speed, consistency, and training, as well as to coordinate appeals procedures.[19]

As a result of these and more recent policy actions, today most biomedical studies in the United Kingdom go through a National Health Service–sponsored central booking service, to be assigned to one of fewer than 100 government-administered review committees, composed of a mix of expert and lay members.[20] The health department supplies these committees with a regularly updated, comprehensive set of standard operating procedures, more than 300 pages in length, and providing guidance—in everyday, non-legalistic language—on how committees should operate.[21] There is also a separate system of university-based ethics boards for social and humanities studies, which is not under the umbrella of health department policies.[22]

The British experience suggests that there are significant advantages to state-coordinated ethics review. Most obviously, it solves the problem of multisite studies. Whereas inconsistent decisions were once endemic in the United Kingdom, today the problem is nonexistent: a clinical trial involving ten different institutions goes through the single, nationwide portal to get on the schedule of a government-coordinated committee with the requisite expertise. Centralization saves time and effort for investigators, who benefit from standardized applications and templates, transparent policies, and predictable outcomes. It creates economies of scale, reducing administrative costs overall. In addition to these efficiency advantages, centralization provides a way to make timely, nationwide decisions about a shifting array of ethical dilemmas. For example, the U.K. Health Department's standard operating procedures for ethics committees contain guidelines for how to handle specific issues associated with gene therapy, tissue banks, and databases containing personal information. These guidelines are frequently updated by senior department staff to reflect changing laws, policy, and expert recommendations.[23] As novel ethical problems emerge, British review committees are not required to wrestle with them alone.

In the United States, problems nearly identical to those resolved by the British reforms were also debated during the 1990s.[24] Here, however, policy solutions were stymied by unamenable institutions and inhospitable politics. Because the U.S. government lacked a powerful national health bureaucracy to use as a foundation (as it was in the United Kingdom), a more consolidated system would have to be created by legislation. But with so many lawmakers congenitally opposed to strengthening state capacity, it was impossible to build a coalition that could overcome the strong headwinds of organized interest groups. The attempt of Senator Kennedy and his allies in the House to pass legislation in 2002 failed, unable to gain support from either congressional Republicans or the Bush administration. More than a decade later, a more modest effort to revise the Common Rule also encountered significant hurdles. Reforms had to be negotiated with more powerful offices within the Department of Health and Human Services (DHHS) and pass through grueling negotiations with parallel government agencies over which OHRP had no authority. The process was also encumbered by layers of rules designed to constrain executive power, including two rounds of public notices and comments (each followed by hundreds of pages of dense agency response) and multiple checkpoints imposed by the Office of Management and Budget.[25] In the end, this harrowing process—which took more than five years—yielded a rather unimposing set of regulatory changes.

With comprehensive policy reform blocked, the United States has, since the federal crackdown, developed private solutions: compliance bureaucracy (including a profitable independent IRB industry), professionalization, and accreditation. This privatized framework can be viewed as a workaround—a structure that has accreted to bypass systemic breakdowns that cannot be addressed more directly. It is better to have a workaround system than a broken one. However, workarounds may deliver suboptimal results, and also unintentionally create new sorts of problems.

One suboptimal feature is the system's very high administrative costs. As a form of enforced self-regulation,[26] the current framework relies on thousands of privately financed compliance bureaucracies, each with one, five, or sometimes even dozens of skilled staff members. Each functions as a quasi-autonomous domain—following the regulations, but also writing and rewriting its own policies, templates, and forms, interpreting regulatory gray areas, and maintaining a voluminous auditable record for inspection by regulators and accreditors. In contrast, under the British system, administrators are far fewer in number—partly because there are far fewer boards to administer, but also because government involvement is more direct, and because policies, templates, and forms are developed and updated by the Health Department.

A second problematic feature is diffuse accountability. Because of their complex, multilayered structure, systems that delegate government functions often lack transparent lines of authority that show "who's in charge"; and the objects of policy often misrecognize "who they're dealing with." Local policies or best practices may be taken for federal regulations; conversely, the role of government may be veiled entirely.[27] In the IRB system the confusion between public and private governance is further complicated by a third layer—the layer of peer ethics review—and a division of labor that can obscure what decisions were made, by whom, and for what reason. When instructed by the IRB office to make changes to a protocol, a researcher may not understand whether it is a matter of regulatory compliance, the ethical judgment of a board member, organizational policy, or simply a discretionary choice by an office staff member. If she believes that the decision is mistaken, it is often unclear how to proceed.[28] Many or most IRBs still lack an appeals mechanism; and, where such mechanisms exist, it appears that they generally apply only to convened full board decisions—and not to the far more numerous everyday decisions with which investigators are asked to comply.[29]

To these disorders, the American framework offers a partial remedy: market incentives that press IRBs toward greater efficiency and better services for investigators. This responsiveness to market signals is most visible in independent IRBs, but has also been gathering force in traditional IRBs that rely on sponsor fees for their operational revenues and that compete with the independents for protocols. In a system where investigators and sponsors are increasingly exercising consumer choice, boards that charge excessive fees, that lack transparency, or that have a reputation for making slow or capricious decisions, are penalized—by decreased revenue streams, reduced operating costs, and perhaps in some cases by having to shut down entirely.

Yet this market workaround, although ingenious, addresses the underlying issues incompletely—and also creates a new set of problems. The cost savings from the competitive market in ethics review services are inherently limited by a structure containing thousands of IRBs, both traditional and independent, each replicating the functions of all the others. Independent boards, which set the pace in the biomedical field, are required to turn a profit for their shareholders, and charge sizable fees. In 2018, the base cost for an initial single review by WIRB-Copernicus, the largest of the independents, was $1,864, with an additional charge of $1,076 per principal investigator and $499 for each additional consent form. Under this fee schedule, a study with three co–principal investigators and one consent form would be charged $5,591 (excluding continuing review).[30] Many principal investigators and sponsors clearly find this to be an acceptable price for rapid review with minimum hassle. As a matter of policy, however, we might ask whether there is a more cost-effective way to protect human subjects.

Most biomedical investigators would almost certainly agree that since the dark days of hypercompliance, IRBs have become more efficient and responsive to investigator concerns. Today's IRB service marketplace responds to the demands of contract research organizations and grant recipients who have money to spend on IRB services and the mobility to take their money elsewhere. Yet there remain many thousands of investigators who are unable to exercise this kind of consumer power: unfunded researchers, often in the social sciences and humanities, who are locked into their own local boards. Thanks to the flexibility movement, many IRB offices have become more sympathetic to the concerns of these researchers. In a system that awards enormous discretion to local authorities, however, there is no guarantee that social and humanities studies will be treated flexibly. Ironically, whereas a contract research organization (CRO) overseeing a risky biomedical experiment may be treated as a valued client, an unfunded anthropologist who wants to do participant observation may be put through the third degree.

Meanwhile, there is the risk that the same market forces that make IRBs more responsive to investigators may also make them less protective of human subjects. Sponsored biomedical researchers and CROs occupy a dual role: they are both the objects of regulation and the financial patrons of the IRBs charged with regulating them. This raises the specter of regulatory capture, and has led some observers to worry that independent boards may, in their haste to satisfy their clients, let problematic research slip through.[31] Such omissions need not imply nefarious intent; they could arise unintentionally, as a result of fierce competition to provide rapid reviews, combined with pressures to cut costs. The audits of AAHRPP—the accreditor that compensates for limited federal oversight—are famously painstaking and thorough, and time may prove that these private standards can withstand the corrosive effects of market incentives. However, the concern remains—and this concern is nonexistent in centralized systems, such as that of the United Kingdom, where there is no private market in ethics review services.

The Virtues of Workaround Protections

Despite these risks, the market-driven, privatized American model must be credited with some important benefits. Remarkably, as this book goes to press there has been no new outbreak of biomedical research scandals since the turn of the twenty-first century. This is in spite of the fact that the United States has remained the international leader in biomedical research, an increasingly commercialized field growing at breakneck speed. The apparent scarcity of lethal research misdeeds is particularly notable in light of the fact that audits conducted by OHRP, the office overseeing federally funded research, have dwindled to practically nothing.[32] For all of its limitations, the system has succeeded in staying out of the headlines.

An equally significant benefit is the system's hardy adaptation to the hardships of the American political climate. This book goes to press during the term of President Donald J. Trump, a famous foe of government regulation, who promised on the campaign trail to "cut so much your head will spin."[33]

True to his word, and with enthusiastic support from congressional Republicans, Trump placed federal agencies under the leadership of regulatory foes who rolled back rules in a wide variety of areas, including environmental protections, worker health and safety, and consumer protections. Some federal agencies, such as the Environmental Protection Agency, saw their budgets significantly reduced. Both the Food and Drug Administration and its parent organization, the Department of Health and Human Services, were placed under the leadership of pharmaceutical industry insiders.[34] According to some of my informants, OHRP's annual budget was being held below inflation and its staff moved to a smaller, windowless suite to reduce costs.

Yet the astonishing thing about the American regulation of human research ethics is that even if OHRP and relevant FDA offices were to suffer grievous budget cuts, the system would likely go on more or less unaffected, at least in the short run. Financed by local institutions and private research dollars, boards would continue to consider ethical and regulatory issues; IRB professionals would continue to develop and apply best practices; and private accreditors would continue to set standards and conduct site visits. A system embedded in private money, standards, and oversight would hum along as usual.

The limited capacity of our federal institutions and the lack of political support for strengthening them are enduring sources of frustration to American progressives. Attempts to use government to address important social issues are thwarted by insurmountable obstacles; hard-won policy victories are often hobbled by compromise; and much-needed reforms are often blocked by unfavorable politics and unamenable institutions. This sometimes puts us in the uncomfortable position of defending suboptimal policy systems, because the alternative would be far worse. In the case of our protections for human research subjects, it is important to clearly understand the imperfections—but also to acknowledge that our workaround framework is a great deal better than nothing. In this day and age, there is something to be said for that.

Appendix: Research Informants

My interviews for this study were semistructured, and mostly conducted by telephone with individuals working for a wide variety of organizations across the country between 2014 and 2018. Many agreed to be interviewed more than once.

To locate informants, I used an eclectic array of sampling techniques. Many of my initial interviewees were individuals who had been interviewed by the trade journal *IRB Advisor*, which provided me with a natural opening to contact them. As my sample size grew, I was able to rely more on existing informants to help put me in touch with other informants (snowball sampling). Although my sample includes both "thought leaders" and everyday practitioners in the IRB world, it is somewhat skewed toward the former, who were better known and more likely to agree to be interviewed. It is also skewed toward individuals working at research institutions rather than liberal arts colleges.

Three of my informants were former federal regulators who agreed to be identified by name. The rest are listed by pseudonym. Although I have listed employment information current at time of the interview, many had occupied other kinds of roles in the IRB world.

Former Federal Regulators

Michael Carome, OPRR/OHRP, 1997–2003
George Gasparis, OPRR/OHRP, 1995–2003
Tom Puglisi, OPRR/OHRP, 1989–2000

Other Informants

Pseudonym	Employer Type	Position Type
Alan	Academic medical center	Research compliance office director
Amanda	Research university	IRB administrator
Amy	Research university	IRB administrator
Andrea	Independent IRB	Administrator
Anna	Research university	IRB administrator
Annie	Research university	Research compliance office director
Beatriz	Research university	IRB administrator
Brian	Compliance consulting firm	Associate
Charles	Research university	Research compliance office director
Claire	Research university	Research administrator
Craig	Compliance consulting firm	Associate
Daphne	Research university	Research compliance office director
David	Liberal arts college	IRB faculty chairperson
Diane	Research university	IRB administrator
Edward	Academic medical center	Research compliance office and IRB director
Elizabeth	Research university	Research compliance office director
Ellen	Research university	IRB administrator
Erin	Research university	IRB administrator
Eve	Research university	IRB administrator
Frances	Independent IRB	Executive officer
Griffin	Research university	IRB faculty chairperson (recently retired)
Gustavo	Research university	IRB administrator

Pseudonym	Employer Type	Position Type
Harold	Academic medical center	IRB administrator
Harriet	Research university	IRB administrator
Howard	Research university	Research compliance office director
Iris	Research university	IRB administrator (retired)
Jacqueline	Nonprofit organization	Director
Janice	Academic medical center	Research compliance office director
Jean	Research university	Research compliance office assistant director
Judith	Research university	IRB administrator
Juliet	Academic medical center	Research compliance office director
Katrina	Academic medical center	Research compliance office director
Kimberly	Research university	IRB administrator
Lara	Research university	IRB administrator
Madeline	Liberal arts college	IRB administrator
Maria	Research university	Research compliance office director
Meghan	Research university	Research compliance office director
Natasha	Research university	Research administrator (retired)
Nicholas	Compliance consulting firm	Associate
Owen	Research university	IRB administrator
Peter	Compliance consulting firm	Associate
Sarah	Compliance consulting firm	Associate
Sean	Research university	Research compliance office director
Sharlene	Research university	IRB administrator
Sheila	Research university	Research compliance office director

Pseudonym	Employer Type	Position Type
Sophia	Research university	IRB administrator
Stephen	Government agency	Research compliance office director
Tamara	Nonprofit organization	Former PRIM&R office-holder
Tanya	Research university	Research compliance office director
Vivian	Health care network	IRB administrator
William	Liberal arts college	IRB administrator

Notes

Introduction

1. DeNeen L. Brown, "'You've Got Bad Blood': The Horror of the Tuskegee Syphilis Experiment," *Washington Post*, May 16, 2017, https://www.washingtonpost.com /news/retropolis/wp/2017/05/16/youve-got-bad-blood-the-horror-of-the-tuskegee -syphilis-experiment/?utm_term=.2e00b1414b2f.

2. Carl Schneider, *The Censor's Hand: The Misregulation of Human-Subject Research* (New York: New York University Press, 2015); Robert Klitzman, *The Ethics Police? The Struggle to Make Human Research Safe* (Oxford: Oxford University Press, 2015); Laura Abbott and Christine Grady, "A Systematic Review of the Empirical Literature Evaluating IRBs: What We Know and What We Still Need to Learn," *Journal of Empirical Research on Human Research Ethics* 6 (2011): 3–20; Malcolm M. Feeley, "Legality, Social Research, and the Challenge of Institutional Review Boards," *Law & Society Review* 41, no. 4 (2007): 757–76; Maureen H. Fitzgerald, "Punctuated Equilibrium, Moral Panics and the Ethics Review Process," *Journal of Academic Ethics* 2 (2004): 315–38; Tara Star Johnson, "Qualitative Research in Question: A Narrative of Disciplinary Power with/in the IRB," *Qualitative Inquiry* 14, no. 2 (2008): 212–32; Caroline H. Bledsoe et al., "Regulating Creativity: Research and Survival in the IRB Iron Cage," *Northwestern University Law Review* 101, no. 2 (2007): 593–641; Laura Jeanine Morris Stark, *Behind Closed Doors: IRBs and the Making of Ethical Research* (Chicago: University of Chicago Press, 2012), 229.

3. Jeanne L. Speckman et al., "Determining the Costs of Institutional Review Boards," *IRB: Ethics and Human Research* 29, no. 2 (2007): 7–13.

4. Public Responsibility in Medicine and Research (PRIM&R), "Workload and Salary Survey, 2007," https://www.primr.org/wlss/ (accessed June 29, 2017).

5. These exceptions include employees of IRBs located within federal agencies such as the U.S. Department of Veterans Affairs or the National Institutes of Health. However, these individuals act as agents of regulated organizations rather than as regulatory officials.

6. Elisabeth S. Clemens, "Lineages of the Rube Goldberg State: Building and Blurring Public Programs, 1900–1940," in *Rethinking Political Institutions: The Art of the State*, ed. Stephen Skowronek and Daniel Galvin (New York: New York University Press, 2006), 188.

7. Brian Balogh, *The Associational State: American Governance in the Twentieth Century* (Philadelphia: University of Pennsylvania Press, 2015); Clemens, "Lineages of the Rube Goldberg State"; Sean Farhang, *The Litigation State: Public Regulation and Private Lawsuits in the United States* (Princeton, NJ: Princeton University Press, 2010).

8. Kimberly J. Morgan and Andrea Louise Campbell, "Delegated Governance in the Affordable Care Act," *Journal of Health Politics, Policy and Law* 36, no. 3 (2011): 387–91; Paul Starr, *Remedy and Reaction: The Peculiar American Struggle over Health Care Reform* (New Haven, CT: Yale University Press, 2011).

9. Thomas Medvetz, *Think Tanks in America* (Chicago: University of Chicago Press, 2012); Sarah Lehman Quinn, "Government Policy, Housing, and the Origins of Securitization, 1780–1968" (PhD diss., University of California, Berkeley, 2010).

10. Byron E. Price and Norma M. Riccucci, "Exploring the Determinants of Decisions to Privatize State Prisons," *American Review of Public Administration* 35, no. 3 (2005): 223–35.

11. Andrea Louise Campbell and Kimberly J. Morgan, *The Delegated Welfare State: Medicare, Markets, and the Governance of Social Policy* (New York: Oxford University Press, 2011); Clemens, "Lineages of the Rube Goldberg State"; Quinn, "Government Policy, Housing, and the Origins of Securitization."

12. Clemens, "Lineages of the Rube Goldberg State," 189; Campbell and Morgan, *The Delegated Welfare State*; Colin D. Moore, "State Building through Partnership: Delegation, Public-Private Partnerships, and the Political Development of American Imperialism, 1898–1916," *Studies in American Political Development* 25, no. 1 (2011): 27–55.

13. Lauren B. Edelman, "Legal Ambiguity and Symbolic Structures: Organizational Mediation of Civil Rights Law," *American Journal of Sociology* 97, no. 6 (1992): 1531–76; Frank Dobbin and John R. Sutton, "The Rights Revolution and the Rise of Human Resources Management Divisions," *American Journal of Sociology* 104, no. 2 (1998): 441–76.

14. Elizabeth Brennan, "Constructing Risk and Legitimizing Place: Privacy Professionals' Interpretation and Implementation of HIPAA in Hospitals" (paper presented

at the annual meetings of the American Sociological Association, Seattle, WA, August 2016); Edelman, "Legal Ambiguity and Symbolic Structures"; Dobbin and Sutton, "The Rights Revolution"; Frank Dobbin, *Inventing Equal Opportunity* (Princeton, NJ: Princeton University Press, 2009). For a general discussion of bureaucracy as an organizational response to regulation, see Ruthanne Huising and Susan S. Silbey, "From Nudge to Culture and Back Again," *Annual Review of Law and Social Science* 14 (2018): 91–114.

15. Edelman, "Legal Ambiguity and Symbolic Structures," 1537; Dobbin, *Inventing Equal Opportunity*.

16. Dobbin, *Inventing Equal Opportunity*; Lauren B. Edelman et al., "When Organizations Rule: Judicial Deference to Institutionalized Employment Structures," *American Journal of Sociology* 117, no. 3 (2011): 888–954; C. Elizabeth Hirsh, "The Strength of Weak Enforcement: The Impact of Discrimination Charges, Legal Environments, and Organizational Conditions on Workplace Segregation," *American Sociological Review* 74, no. 2 (2009): 245–71.

17. For an analysis of privacy officers in the United States, Canada, and France, see Kartikeya Bajpai, "Cross-National Variation in Occupational Prestige," *Academy of Management Proceedings* 2017, no. 1 (2017): 1.

18. Maureen H. Fitzgerald and Paul A. Phillips, "Centralized and Non-centralized Ethics Review: A Five Nation Study," *Accountability in Research* 13, no. 1 (2006): 47–74; Rustam Al-Shahi Salman et al., "Increasing Value and Reducing Waste in Biomedical Research Regulation and Management," *The Lancet* 383, no. 9912 (2014): 176–85; Stuart G. Nicholls et al., "Call for a Pan-Canadian Approach to Ethics Review in Canada," *Canadian Medical Association Journal* 190, no. 18 (2018): E553–55.

19. The Canadian and Australian systems are the ones most similar to the American IRB framework. Fitzgerald and Phillips, "Centralized and Non-centralized Ethics Review," 47–74.

20. A. Hedgecoe et al., "Research Ethics Committees in Europe: Implementing the Directive, Respecting Diversity," *Journal of Medical Ethics* 32, no. 8 (August 2006): 483–86; Delphine Stoffel et al., *Ethics Assessment in Different Countries: France* (European Commission, 2015), http://satoriproject.eu/media/4.d-Country-report-France.pdf.

21. Edelman, "Legal Ambiguity and Symbolic Structures," 1542; Alexandra Kalev, Frank Dobbin, and Erin Kelly, "Best Practices or Best Guesses? Assessing the Efficacy of Corporate Affirmative Action and Diversity Policies," *American Sociological Review* 71, no. 4 (2006): 589–617; Dobbin, *Inventing Equal Opportunity*, 86.

22. Jeanne L. Speckman et al., "Determining the Costs of Institutional Review Boards," *IRB: Ethics & Human Research* 29, no. 2 (2007): 7–13.

23. WIRB-Copernicus Group, "2018 Single Review Service Fee Schedule" (Princeton, NJ: WIRB-Copernicus, 2018).

24. Max Weber, *Economy and Society: An Outline of Interpretive Sociology*, trans. Guenther Roth and Claus Wittich (Berkeley: University of California Press, 1978), 973.

25. Edelman, "Legal Ambiguity and Symbolic Structures."

26. Dobbin, *Inventing Equal Opportunity*.

27. Sharona Hoffman and Jessica Wilen Berg, "The Suitability of IRB Liability," *University of Pittsburgh Law Review* 67 (2005): 365.

28. Following Michael Power, I use the term "audit" in the broad sense, to refer to any formal assessment by an independent body to hold an organization accountable. See Michael Power, *The Audit Society: Rituals of Verification* (New York: Oxford University Press, 1997).

29. Kristina Borror et al., "A Review of OHRP Compliance Oversight Letters," *IRB: Ethics and Human Research* 25, no. 5 (2003): 1–4; Scott Burris and Jen Welsh, "Regulatory Paradox: A Review of Enforcement Letters Issued by the Office for Human Research Protection," *Northwestern University Law Review* 101, no. 2 (2007): 643.

30. Bledsoe et al., "Regulating Creativity."

31. Weber, *Economy and Society*, 975.

Chapter 1: The Federal Crackdown and the Twilight of Approximate Compliance

1. U.S. Department of Health and Human Services, Office of the Inspector General, *Institutional Review Boards: A Time for Reform* (Washington, DC: U.S. Department of Health and Human Services, 1998), appendix C.

2. See Stark, *Behind Closed Doors*, 83.

3. Ibid.

4. Charles R. McCarthy, "The Origins and Policies That Govern Institutional Review Boards," in *The Oxford Textbook of Clinical Research Ethics*, ed. Ezekiel J. Emmanuel et al. (New York: Oxford University Press, 2008), 50–75.

5. At that time, the parent agency was the Department of Health, Education and Welfare. FDA began requiring IRB review in 1969. See Daniel P. Carpenter, *Reputation and Power: Organizational Image and Pharmaceutical Regulation at the FDA* (Princeton, NJ: Princeton University Press, 2010).

6. McCarthy, "The Origins and Policies That Govern Institutional Review Boards."

7. See U.S. Congress, Senate, Committee on Labor and Public Welfare, Subcommittee on Health, *Quality of Health Care—Human Experimentation, 1973. Hearings, Ninety-Third Congress, First Session, on S. 974* (Washington, DC: Government Printing Office, 1973), 1659.

8. See Hedgecoe et al., "Research Ethics Committees in Europe"; Patricia Jaspers, Rob Houtepen, and Klasien Horstman, "Ethical Review: Standardizing Procedures and Local Shaping of Ethical Review Practices," *Social Science & Medicine* 98 (2013): 311–18; Stoffel et al., *Ethics Assessment in Different Countries: France*.

9. U.S. Congress, House, Committee on Interstate and Foreign Commerce, *Biomedical Research Ethics and the Protection of Human Research Subjects: Hearings before the Subcommittee on Public Health and Environment of the Committee on Interstate and Foreign Commerce, House of Representatives, Ninety-Third Congress, First Session . . . September 27 and 28, 1973* (Washington, DC: Government Printing Office, 1974), 292.

10. Sydney Halpern, "Hybrid Design, Systemic Rigidity: Institutional Dynamics in Human Research Oversight," *Regulation & Governance* 2, no. 1 (2008): 85–102.

11. Ibid.; Mark Steven Frankel, "Public Policymaking for Biomedical Research: The Case of Human Experimentation" (PhD diss., George Washington University, 1976).

12. Ibid., 275–76.

13. Assistant Secretary of U.S. Department of Health, Education and Welfare Merlin K. Duval, interview in ibid., 177.

14. See R. Shep Melnick, "From Tax and Spend to Mandate and Sue: Liberalism after the Great Society," in *The Great Society and the High Tide of Liberalism*, ed. Sidney M. Milkis and Jerome M. Mileur (Amherst, MA: University of Massachusetts Press, 2005), 387–410; Farhang, *The Litigation State*.

15. Interview with former OPRR official Tom Puglisi, June 22, 2016.

16. "Protection of Human Subjects," Code of Federal Regulations, Title 45, Part 46 (1981).

17. For example, the concept of "exemption" was added to the 1981 regulations in response to the concerns of social and behavioral researchers. To get buy-in from the Department of Agriculture, the 1991 Common Rule included language exempting "taste and food quality evaluation and consumer acceptance studies." See Zachary M. Schrag, *Ethical Imperialism: Institutional Review Boards and the Social Sciences, 1965–2009* (Baltimore: Johns Hopkins University Press, 2010); J. Porter and Greg Koski, "Regulations for the Protection of Humans in Research in the United States," in *The Oxford Textbook of Clinical Research Ethics*, ed. Ezekiel J. Emmanuel et al. (New York: Oxford University Press, 2008, 156–67.

18. National Bioethics Advisory Commission, *Ethical and Policy Issues in Research Involving Human Participants*, vol. 1 (Bethesda, MD: National Bioethics Advisory Commission, 2001).

19. In 1999 OPRR had a budget of only $2.6 million—compared to the $15.6 billion budget of NIH, the entity whose research it was ostensibly regulating. Daniel S. Greenberg, *Science for Sale: The Perils, Rewards, and Delusions of Campus Capitalism* (Chicago: University of Chicago Press, 2007), 134.

20. U.S. Congress, House, Committee on Government Reform and Oversight, Subcommittee on Human Resources, *Institutional Review Boards, a System in Jeopardy: Hearing before the Subcommittee on Human Resources of the Committee on*

Government Reform and Oversight, House of Representatives, One Hundred Fifth Congress, Second Session, June 11, 1998 (Washington, DC: Government Printing Office), 55–56.

21. McCarthy notes that the education budget was not reinstated during the Clinton administration; see Charles R. McCarthy, "Reflections on the Organizational Locus of the Office for Protection from Research Risks," in National Bioethics Advisory Commission, *Ethical and Policy Issues in Research Involving Human Participants*, vol. 2 (Bethesda, MD: National Bioethics Advisory Commission, 2001), http://www.onlineethics.org/cms/17252.aspx.

22. U.S. General Accounting Office, *Scientific Research: Continued Vigilance Critical to Protecting Human Subjects* (Washington, DC: U.S. General Accounting Office, 1996).

23. Greenberg, *Science for Sale*.

24. R. A. Rettig, "The Industrialization of Clinical Research," *Health Affairs* 19, no. 2 (March–April 2000): 129–46; Mirowski and Van Horn, "The Contract Research Organization."

25. Jeannette Anastasia Colyvas, "From Divergent Meanings to Common Practices: Institutionalization Processes and the Commercialization of University Research" (PhD diss., Stanford University, 2007); Elizabeth Popp Berman, *Creating the Market University: How Academic Science Became an Economic Engine* (Princeton, NJ: Princeton University Press, 2011).

26. Quoted in U.S. Congress, House, Committee on Government Reform and Oversight, Subcommittee on Human Resources, *Institutional Review Boards*, 2.

27. U.S. General Accounting Office, *Scientific Research*.

28. National Bioethics Advisory Commission, *Ethical and Policy Issues in Research Involving Human Participants*, vol. 1, 4.

29. U.S. Department of Health and Human Services, Office of Inspector General, *Protecting Human Research Subjects: Status of Recommendations* (Washington, DC: U.S. Department of Health and Human Services, 2000).

30. U.S. General Accounting Office, *Scientific Research*.

31. Thomas O. Stair et al., "Variation in Institutional Review Board Responses to a Standard Protocol for a Multicenter Clinical Trial," *Academic Emergency Medicine* 8, no. 6 (2001): 636–41; Henry Silverman, Sara Chandros Hull, and Jeremy Sugarman, "Variability among Institutional Review Boards' Decisions within the Context of a Multicenter Trial," *Critical Care Medicine* 29, no. 2 (2001): 235–41.

32. Ellis testimony in U.S., Congress, House, Committee on Small Business, Subcommittee on Regulation, Business Opportunities, and Technology, *Problems in Securing Informed Consent of Subjects in Experimental Trials of Unapproved Drugs and Devices: Hearing before the Subcommittee on Regulation, Business Opportunities, and Technology of the Committee on Small Business, House of Representatives, One*

Hundred Third Congress, Second Session, Washington, DC, May 23, 1994 (Washington, DC: Government Printing Office), 58.

33. Sheryl Gay Stolberg, "Teenager's Death Is Shaking Up Field of Human Gene-Therapy Experiments," *New York Times*, January 27, 2001; Elisabeth Rosenthal, "New York Seeks to Tighten Rules on Medical Research," *New York Times*, September 7, 1996; Philip J. Hilts, "Agency Faults a U.C.L.A. Study for Suffering of Mental Patients," *New York Times*, March 10, 1994.

34. U.S. Department of Health and Human Services, Office of the Inspector General, *Protecting Human Research Subjects*. OPRR's successor agency, OHRP, made two additional suspensions over the three years that followed; see Greg Koski, "Beyond Compliance . . . Is It Too Much to Ask?," *IRB: Ethics & Human Research* 25, no. 5 (2002): 5–6.

35. J. Brainard, "Spate of Suspensions of Academic Research Spurs Questions about Federal Strategy: A U.S. Agency, Its Own Future Uncertain, Unsettles College Officials with Its Crackdown," *Chronicle of Higher Education*, February 4, 2000, A29–30, A32.

36. Borror et al., "A Review of OHRP Compliance Oversight Letters."

37. Burris and Welsh, "Regulatory Paradox," 643.

38. Ellis, quoted in Greenberg, *Science for Sale*.

39. National Bioethics Advisory Commission, *Ethical and Policy Issues in Research Involving Human Participants*, vol. 1.

40. Power, *The Audit Society*.

41. As Charles McCarthy, the OPRR director who oversaw the update, later recalled: "Without adequate records it was often impossible to develop clear findings of noncompliance . . . and to impose sanctions on institutions or investigators who were noncompliant. These shortcomings were corrected in the 1981 version of the rules." McCarthy, "Reflections on the Organizational Locus of the Office for Protection from Research Risks," 5.

42. In the process, director Gary Ellis was forced to step down. One former OPRR official informed me that this was a deliberate move to get rid of an official whose regulatory actions were viewed by NIH as overzealous.

43. U.S. Department of Health and Human Services, Office of the Inspector General, *Protecting Human Research Subjects*; U.S. General Accounting Office, *Scientific Research*.

44. NBAC was one of a series of bioethics advisory commissions dating back to the original National Commission established in 1974. NBAC was established by executive order in 1995. Its charter expired in 2001, when it was succeeded by the President's Council on Bioethics.

45. National Bioethics Advisory Commission, *Ethical and Policy Issues in Research Involving Human Participants*, vol. 1, xii, 30.

46. Erin D. Williams, *Federal Protection for Human Research Subjects: An Analysis of the Common Rule and Its Interactions with FDA Regulations and the HIPAA Privacy Rule* (Washington, DC: Congressional Research Service, 2005).

47. McCarthy, "Reflections on the Organizational Locus of the Office for the Protection from Research Risks."

48. A parallel bill (H.R. 4697) was introduced in the House of Representatives and similarly died in committee. E. Williams, *Federal Protection for Human Research Subjects*, 11.

49. Steven H. Landers and Ashwini R. Sehgal, "Health Care Lobbying in the United States," *American Journal of Medicine* 116, no. 7 (2004): 474–77.

Chapter 2: Leaving It to the Professionals

1. Tim Hallett, "The Myth Incarnate: Recoupling Processes, Turmoil, and Inhabited Institutions in an Urban Elementary School," *American Sociological Review* 75, no. 1 (2010): 52–74.

2. Janet Heinrich, *Human Subjects Research: HHS Takes Steps to Strengthen Protections, but Concerns Remain* (Washington, DC: U.S. General Accounting Office, 2001), 12.

3. IRB Advisor, "Protocols Involving Oral History Still Need Review," *IRB Advisor* (February 1, 2004); IRB Advisor, "Historians, OHRP and IRBs Looking for Common Ground on Oral History Projects," *IRB Advisor* (March 1, 2006).

4. Koski, "Beyond Compliance."

5. Organizations are famous for responding to uncertainty by buffering themselves against potential risks. See James D. Thompson, *Organizations in Action* (New York: McGraw-Hill, 1967).

6. IRB Advisor, "Special Report: Regulations and Rules—Are We Heading in the Right Direction?," *IRB Advisor* (July 1, 2004).

7. IRB Advisor, "Mission Creep: Is It Leading IRBs Astray?," *IRB Advisor* (April 1, 2006).

8. IRB Advisor, "Teaching IRBs to Be Flexible, Drop Bad Habits," *IRB Advisor* (June 1, 2011).

9. IRB Advisor, "Fairness and Common Sense Can Ease Tensions," *IRB Advisor* (August 1, 2006).

10. Schrag, *Ethical Imperialism*.

11. Elizabeth H. Gorman and Rebecca L. Sandefur, "'Golden Age,' Quiescence, and Revival: How the Sociology of Professions Became the Study of Knowledge-Based Work," *Work and Occupations* 38, no. 3 (2011): 275–302.

12. Public Responsibility in Medicine and Research (PRIM&R), "Membership Data," unpublished internal database (2019).

13. See Sarah L. Babb, *Managing Mexico: Economists from Nationalism to Neoliberalism* (Princeton, NJ: Princeton University Press, 2001).

14. Jeffrey Brainard, "NIH, FDA Should Do More to Protect Human Subjects in Research, Report Says," *Chronicle of Higher Education* 46, no. 33, April 21, 2000, https://www.chronicle.com/article/NIH-FDA-Should-Do-More-to/19529 (accessed May 31, 2019). See also Greenberg, *Science for Sale.*

15. Todd H. Wagner et al., "The Cost of Operating Institutional Review Boards (IRBs)," *Academic Medicine* 78, no. 6 (2003): 638–44.

16. Koski, "Beyond Compliance," 5.

17. Public Responsibility in Medicine and Research (PRIM&R), "Workload and Salary Survey."

18. PricewaterhouseCoopers hired former regulators to serve on these consulting teams, and in early 2001 published an IRB reference book advertised as "the most current and comprehensive compilation of government documents, guidance and resources available," priced at $295. See PricewaterhouseCoopers, promotional flyer for *The IRB Reference Book,* http://www.proirb.com/files/IRB%20Ref.Book%20Flyer3 -11.16.01.pdf (accessed October 6, 2017).

19. Ellis, quoted in Greenberg, *Science for Sale.*

20. Borror et al., "A Review of OHRP Compliance Oversight Letters"; Burris and Welsh, "Regulatory Paradox," 643.

21. Passed in 1996, the act's main purpose was to improve access to health insurance. Because it placed restrictions on the use of private health information in research, IRBs were required to act as "privacy boards" that reviewed research involving health information to determine whether the act and related regulations were being upheld.

22. IRB Advisor, "Spotlight on Compliance: Is Data Collection Research? It Depends: OHRP Clarifies Use of Data in Research," *IRB Advisor* (October 1, 2004).

23. IRB Advisor, "Reporting Rules for Adverse Events, Unanticipated Problems Differ Slightly," *IRB Advisor* (March 1, 2004).

24. Delano, interviewed in IRB Advisor, "IRB Certification Becomes Industry Gold Standard," *IRB Advisor* (October 1, 2010).

25. Ibid.

26. Ibid. See also IRB Advisor, "2003 Salary Survey Results," *IRB Advisor* (November 1, 2003); IRB Advisor, "CIP Certification Is Taking Off among IRB Staff," *IRB Advisor* (July 1, 2006).

27. Dobbin and Sutton, "The Rights Revolution"; Kim Pernell, Jiwook Jung, and Frank Dobbin, "The Hazards of Expert Control: Chief Risk Officers and Risky Derivatives," *American Sociological Review* 82, no. 3 (2017): 511–41; Hirsh, "The Strength of Weak Enforcement."

28. PRIM&R originally became a formal not-for-profit organization in 1979, in the wake of the passage of the National Research Act, the promulgation of the regulations, and the drafting of the Belmont Report. Public Responsibility in Medicine and Research (PRIM&R), "History," http://www.primr.org/about/history/ (accessed October 14, 2016).

29. In 1983, PRIM&R began to host an annual conference on the use of animals in research, corresponding to Institutional Animal Care and Use Committees (IACUCs). The organization has hosted separate IRB and IACUC conferences ever since, but the IRB section is the dominant of the two. Many members participate in both. Ibid.

30. Lawrence W. Green, "From Research to 'Best Practices' in Other Settings and Populations," *American Journal of Health Behavior* 25, no. 3 (2001): 165–78.

31. For parallel observations in the field of equal employment opportunity, see Edelman, "Legal Ambiguity and Symbolic Structures"; Dobbin and Sutton, "The Rights Revolution"; Dobbin, *Inventing Equal Opportunity*.

32. Donna Shalala, "Protecting Research Subjects: What Must Be Done," *New England Journal of Medicine* 343, no. 11 (2000): 808–10.

33. Schrag, *Ethical Imperialism*, 139; Collaborative Institutional Training Initiative (CITI), "Management Team," https://about.citiprogram.org/en/leadership/ (accessed October 6, 2017).

34. Collaborative Institutional Training Initiative (CITI), "Mission and History," https://about.citiprogram.org/en/mission-and-history/ (accessed October 6, 2017); Paul Braunschweiger and Kenneth W. Goodman, "The CITI Program: An International Online Resource for Education in Human Subjects Protection and the Responsible Conduct of Research," *Academic Medicine* 82 (2007): 861–64.

35. Biomedical Research Alliance of New York (BRANY), "BRANY Announces Acquisition of University of Miami's CITI Program," http://www.brany.com/2016/05/13/brany-announces-acquisition-university-miamis-citi-collaborative-institutional-training-initiative-program/ (accessed October 6, 2017). Although CITI was founded as a not-for-profit organization, it also generated considerable revenue: the annual base fee for an organizational subscription in 2017 was $3,500, and $4,000 for not-for-profit and for-profit organizations, respectively—see Collaborative Institutional Training Initiative (CITI), "Organizational Subscriptions," https://about.citiprogram.org/en/organizational-subscriptions/ (accessed October 6, 2017).

36. U.S. National Institutes of Health (NIH), "Protecting Human Research Participants (PHRP) Online Tutorial No Longer Available as of September 26, 2018," https://grants.nih.gov/grants/guide/notice-files/NOT-OD-18-221.html (accessed February 4, 2019).

Chapter 3: Organizing for Efficiency

1. Weber, *Economy and Society*, 975.

2. The results of this study are described in Sara Rockwell, "The FDP Faculty Burden Survey," *Research Management Review* 16, no. 2 (Spring 2009): 29–44.

3. Greenberg, *Science for Sale*, 174.

4. Ibid.

5. One of AAHRPP's two leading cosponsors was the American Association of Medical Colleges—a lobbying organization representing medical school administrators. The second was Public Responsibility in Medicine and Research (PRIM&R). Other founding members included the Consortium of Social Science Associations, the Federation of American Societies for Experimental Biology, the National Association of State Universities and Land Grant Colleges, and the National Health Council. See Halpern, "Hybrid Design, Systemic Rigidity."

6. The accrediting agency that AAHRPP put out of business was the National Committee for Quality Assurance. See Halpern, "Hybrid Design, Systemic Rigidity." A third accreditation service was later launched by the Alion Science and Technology Corporation, but AAHRPP continued to be by far the more influential of the two.

7. Marjorie Speers, quoted in IRB Advisor, "IRB Costs Are Greater than Previous Estimates," *IRB Advisor* (July 1, 2005).

8. Public Responsibility in Medicine and Research (PRIM&R), "Workload and Salary Survey, 2007"; IRB Advisor, "Improve IRB Staffing Issues Following This Good Example," *IRB Advisor* (April 1, 2011); IRB Advisor, "Add Some Climbs and Hills to Typically Flat Career Path," *IRB Advisor* (July 14, 2016).

9. On routines, see Robin Leidner, *Fast Food, Fast Talk: Service Labor and the Routinization of Everyday Life* (Berkeley: University of California Press, 1993).

10. Borror et al., "A Review of OHRP Compliance Oversight Letters."

11. Northwestern University, Office for Research, "SOP Daily Tasks," https://irb .northwestern.edu/sites/irb/files/documents/hrp-062-sop-daily-tasks.pdf (accessed October 20, 2017).

12. For the checklist's function as a "cognitive net," see Atul Gawande, *The Checklist Manifesto: How to Get Things Right* (New York: Picador, 2011).

13. By 2014, two-thirds of respondents in a survey of the IRB world reported that their offices used protocol management software. See Public Responsibility in Medicine and Research (PRIM&R), "Workload and Salary Survey."

14. iMedris, "IRB Software Overview," iMedris, https://imedris.com/Modules/IRB -Software (accessed July 7, 2018).

15. Speckman et al., "Determining the Costs of Institutional Review Boards."

16. IRB Advisor, "Making the Case for a New Electronic System," *IRB Advisor* (November 1, 2010); IRB Advisor, "Baylor Uses Its BRAAN to Improve IRB Opera-

tions," *IRB Advisor* (April 1, 2003); IRB Advisor, "Staffing, Collaborations Top IRB Issues," *IRB Advisor* (January 1, 2014).

17. IRB Advisor, "2008 Salary Survey Results: Economic Woes May Mean Less Hiring, Smaller Raises for IRB Professionals," *IRB Advisor* (January 1, 2009); IRB Advisor, "Managers of IRBs Can Save Time with Tech," *IRB Advisor* (October 1, 2010).

18. IRB Advisor, "Should Administrators Be Voting Members?," *IRB Advisor* (July 1, 2005).

19. This was an artifact of 1995 federal guidance suggesting that exemption determinations should be made by individuals familiar with the regulations.

20. See Jonathan D. Loe, D. Alex Winkelman, and Christopher T. Robertson, "An Assessment of the Human Subjects Protection Review Process for Exempt Research," *Journal of Law, Medicine & Ethics* 44, no. 3 (2016): 481–91.

21. Ronald F. White, "Institutional Review Board Mission Creep: The Common Rule, Social Science, and the Nanny State," *Independent Review* 11, no. 4 (2007): 554; Ivor Pritchard, "How Do IRB Members Make Decisions? A Review and Research Agenda," *Journal of Empirical Research on Human Research Ethics* 6 (2011): 31–46.

22. "Protection of Human Subjects," Code of Federal Regulations, Title 45, Part 46 (1991): sec. 111.

23. See Janice Irvine, "Can't Ask, Can't Tell: How Institutional Review Boards Keep Sex in the Closet," *Contexts* 11 (2012): 28–33.

24. Stark, *Behind Closed Doors*, 83. On bureaucratic versus collegial authority, see Elizabeth A. Boyd, "Bureaucratic Authority in the Company of Equals: The Interactional Management of Medical Peer Review," *American Sociological Review* 63, no. 2 (1998): 200–224.

25. These more bureaucratic requirements did not appear in the 1974 regulations (which were mostly copied from NIH's internal policy), but rather in their 1981 update. See McCarthy, "Reflections on the Organizational Locus of the Office for the Protection from Research Risks"; "Protection of Human Subjects," Code of Federal Regulations, Title 45, Part 46 (1991): secs. 107a and 103b.

26. William G. Tierney and Zoe Blumberg Corwin, "The Tensions between Academic Freedom and Institutional Review Boards," *Qualitative Inquiry* 13, no. 3 (2007): 392.

27. See American Association of University Professors, "Research on Human Subjects: Academic Freedom and the Institutional Review Board," http://www.aaup.org/AAUP/comm/rep/A/humansubs.htm (accessed January 23, 2010).

28. IRB Advisor, "IRB Expert Strategies for Improving PI-IRB Relations," *IRB Advisor* (October 1, 2013).

29. Robert Michels, *Political Parties: A Sociological Study of the Oligarchical Tendencies of Modern Democracy* (New York: Dover Publications, 1959), 34.

30. IRB Advisor, "IC under Revised Common Rule Is Transparent, Tightened," *IRB Advisor* (November 1, 2015); IRB Advisor, "True Simplicity Remains Elusive for IC Forms," *IRB Advisor* (February 1, 2013); IRB Advisor, "IRBs Tie Up Study with Informed Consent Changes," *IRB Advisor* (August 1, 2009); IRB Advisor, "Expert Outlines Main Struggles, Solutions to Better Informed Consent," *IRB Advisor* (September 1, 2009); U.S. Department of Health and Human Services, "Human Subjects Research Protections: Enhancing Protections for Research Subjects and Reducing Burden, Delay, and Ambiguity for Investigators," *Federal Register* 76, no. 143 (2011): 44512–44531.

31. IRB Advisor, "True Simplicity Remains Elusive for IC Forms."

32. Sarah Babb, Lara Birk, and Luka Carfagna, "Standard Bearers: Qualitative Sociologists' Experiences with IRB Regulation," *American Sociologist* 48, no. 1 (2017): 86–102.

Chapter 4: Ethics Review, Inc.

1. I have chosen the term "industrialization" over the more commonly used "commercialization" to refer to a broader shift in the field's structure, practices, and rhetoric. Commercialization—the growing dominance of private money and market forces—can be seen as one of the main causes of industrialization. See Rettig, "The Industrialization of Clinical Research," 129–46.

2. Stephan Ehrhardt, Lawrence J. Appel, and Curtis L. Meinert, "Trends in National Institutes of Health Funding for Clinical Trials Registered in ClinicalTrials.gov," *JAMA* 314, no. 23 (2015): 2566–67.

3. Colyvas, "From Divergent Meanings to Common Practices"; Popp Berman, *Creating the Market University*.

4. Jill Fisher, *Medical Research for Hire: The Political Economy of Pharmaceutical Clinical Trials* (New Brunswick, NJ: Rutgers University Press, 2008).

5. Erica Heath, *The History, Function, and Future of Independent Institutional Review Boards* (Washington, DC: Online Ethics Center, 2000), http://www.onlineethics.org/cms/8080.aspx.

6. Heath, *The History, Function, and Future of Independent Institutional Review Boards*, 9.

7. "Who Watches the Watchmen? Some Commercial Firms that Oversee the Ethics and Scrutiny of Clinical Trials Have Been Found Wanting. Human Volunteers in Research Deserve Better," *Nature* 476 (2011): 125.

8. IRB Advisor, "IRB Seals Fate by Approving Fake Protocol in Federal Sting," *IRB Advisor* (July 1, 2009); Rachel Douglas-Jones, "Getting Inside Ethical Review: Anxious Bureaucracies of Revelation, Anticipation and Virtue," *Critical Public Health* 29 (2019): 448–59. As this book goes to press, there has been no sequel to the Coast scandal, which occurred in 2009.

9. IRB Advisor, "Single IRB NIH Guidance May Leave More Questions than Answers," *IRB Advisor* (March 1, 2015).

10. Ronald Rosenberg, "AMCs Vying to Better Compete for Industry Trials: Working to Conquer Study Start-Up Delays, IRB Review Process," *CenterWatch Monthly*, December 2014, sec. 21; Karyn Korieth, "AMCs Show Renewed Interest in Industry Research: New Collaborations, Greater Trust Breaking Down Research Silos," *CenterWatch Monthly*, November 2013, sec. 20.

11. U.S. Department of Health and Human Services, *Human Subjects Research Protections*.

12. Heath, *The History, Function, and Future of Independent Institutional Review Boards*, 3.

13. IRB Advisor, "OHRP Move Might Increase Trend of Research Sites Using Central IRBs," *IRB Advisor* (August 1, 2010).

14. IRB Advisor, "Single IRB NIH Guidance May Leave More Questions than Answers"; Kaplan, "In Clinical Trials, For-Profit Review Boards Are Taking Over."

15. IRB Advisor, "Preparation, Communication Key to Establishing IRB of Record," *IRB Advisor* (April 1, 2018).

16. IRB Advisor, "Experts: NIRB and IRB Share Are Alternatives to Central IRBs," *IRB Advisor* (July 1, 2015); IRB Advisor, "NCI's Central IRB Saves Time, Money," *IRB Advisor* (February 1, 2010).

17. IRB Advisor, "The Changing World of Independent IRBs," *IRB Advisor* (October 1, 2014); IRB Advisor, "Central IRBs: Consistency Increases, but So Does Confusion," *IRB Advisor* (October 1, 2014).

18. Melissa Fassbender, "IRB Consolidation Continues as Chesapeake and Schulman Merge to Form Advarra," *Outsourcing-Pharma.Com*, November 8, 2017, https://www.outsourcing-pharma.com/Article/2017/11/08/Chesapeake-IRB-and-Schulman-IRB-merge-to-form-Advarra.

19. Kaplan, "In Clinical Trials, For-Profit Review Boards Are Taking Over for Hospitals."

20. IRB Advisor, "The Changing World of Independent IRBs."

21. Korieth, "AMCs Show Renewed Interest."

22. Statistic from John Isidor, chief executive officer of Schulman Associates IRB, cited in IRB Advisor, "OHRP Move Might Increase Trend of Research Sites Using Central IRBs," *IRB Advisor* (August 1, 2010).

23. IRB Advisor, "Supply and Demand: IRB Fees Now Are the Norm," *IRB Advisor* (October 1, 2003).

24. Ernest Prentice, Sally L. Mann, and Bruce G. Gordon, "Charging for Institutional Review Board Review," in *Institutional Review Board: Management and*

Function, ed. Elizabeth A. Bankert and Robert J. Amdur, 2nd ed. (Boston: Jones and Bartlett, 2006), 57.

25. Health centers that serve as sites for clinical trials also frequently maintain their own IRBs.

26. IRB Advisor, "Reduce Complaints with New Policies and Procedures," *IRB Advisor* (April 1, 2007).

27. IRB Advisor, "IRB Cuts 35 Days from Protocol Turnaround," *IRB Advisor* (November 1, 2009).

28. IRB Advisor, "The Changing World of Independent IRBs."

29. For example, AAHRPP would certify a university's conflict of interest policy—something that was relevant to human subjects protection but not formally part of IRBs' mandate. The "human research participant protection program" concept made its debut in an OHRP-commissioned study on accreditation authored by the Institute of Medicine. See Institute of Medicine, *Preserving Public Trust*.

30. IRB Advisor, "Accreditation Is Not for the Faint of Heart," *IRB Advisor* (September 1, 2003); Association for the Accreditation of Human Research Protection Programs (AAHRPP), "Application Fees 2017," https://admin.share.aahrpp.org/Website%20Documents/Application%20Fees%202017%20-%20Domestic.pdf (accessed November 16, 2017); Association for the Accreditation of Human Research Protection Programs (AAHRPP), "Accredited Organizations," http://www.aahrpp.org/learn/find-an-accredited-organization (accessed October 16, 2016).

31. Huron Consulting Group, "IRB Transformation Solutions," https://www.huronconsultinggroup.com/-/media/Resource-Media-Content/Education/RES_IRB-Transformation-Sell-Sheet.pdf?la=en (accessed October 22, 2016).

32. Office for Human Research Protections (OHRP), "OHRP's Compliance Oversight Procedures for Evaluating Institutions," http://www.hhs.gov/ohrp/compliance-and-reporting/evaluating-institutions/ (accessed October 13, 2016).

33. Association for the Accreditation of Human Research Protection Programs (AAHRPP), "Pfizer Is First Pharmaceutical Company to Earn Accreditation," http://www.aahrpp.org/apply/web-document-library/pfizer-is-first-pharmaceutical-company-to-earn-accreditation (accessed October 13, 2016).

34. IRB Advisor, "OHRP Move Might Increase Trend of Research Sites Using Central IRBs."

35. Association for the Accreditation of Human Research Protection Programs (AAHRPP), *Accreditation for Human Research Protection Programs* (Washington, DC: AAHRPP, 2017), 4.

36. Curtis P. McLaughlin and Arnold D. Kaluzny, *Continuous Quality Improvement in Health Care: Theory, Implementation, and Applications* (Sudbury, MA: Jones & Bartlett Learning, 2004).

37. John Baumann, IRB executive director, interviewed in IRB Advisor, "Every Improvement Helps IRB Efficiencies," *IRB Advisor* (June 1, 2014).

38. Kalev, Dobbin, and Kelly, "Best Practices or Best Guesses?," 589–617.

39. See IRB Advisor, "New AAHRPP Metrics Show Less IRB Funding," *IRB Advisor* (September 1, 2011).

40. IRB Advisor, "Accreditation Expert Offers Assessment Tips," *IRB Advisor* (May 1, 2014); IRB Advisor, "Data Driven: Accreditation Group Releases Metrics for IRB Performance," *IRB Advisor* (September 1, 2010).

41. IRB Advisor, "Institution's QI Form Serves as Educational Tool for PIs," *IRB Advisor* (November 1, 2007).

42. See Office for Human Research Protections (OHRP), "FWAs," https://ohrp.cit.nih.gov/search/fwasearch.aspx?styp=bsc (accessed November 16, 2017). It is important to note that the OHRP numbers did not include the thousands of IRBs that followed only FDA regulations. There is no publicly-available list of FDA-regulated IRBs, and my Freedom of Information Act request for this information never received a response.

43. Paul J. DiMaggio and Walter W. Powell, "The Iron Cage Revisited: Institutional Isomorphism and Collective Rationality in Organizational Fields," *American Sociological Review* 48, no. 2 (April 1983): 147–60; W. Richard Scott et al., *Institutional Change and Healthcare Organizations: From Professional Dominance to Managed Care* (Chicago: University of Chicago Press, 2000).

44. Public Responsibility in Medicine and Research (PRIM&R), *Program: 2017 Advancing Ethical Research Conference* (Boston: PRIM&R, 2017), 88–92.

Chapter 5: The Common Rule and Social Research

1. Koski, "Beyond Compliance."

2. C. K. Gunsalus et al., "Mission Creep in the IRB World," *Science* 312, no. 5779 (2006): 1441.

3. Schrag, *Ethical Imperialism*.

4. Ibid., 133; Jack Katz, "Toward a Natural History of Ethical Censorship," *Law & Society Review* 41, no. 4 (December 2007): 797–810.

5. Loe, Winkelman, and Robertson, "An Assessment of the Human Subjects Protection Review Process for Exempt Research."

6. See Stuart Plattner, "Human Subjects Protection and Cultural Anthropology," *Anthropological Quarterly* 76, no. 2 (2003): 287–97; Schrag, *Ethical Imperialism*.

7. Rena Lederman, "The Perils of Working at Home: IRB 'Mission Creep' as Context and Content for an Ethnography of Disciplinary Knowledges," *American Ethnologist* 33, no. 4 (2006): 486.

8. National Research Council, *Proposed Revisions to the Common Rule for the Protection of Human Subjects in the Behavioral and Social Sciences* (Washington, DC: National Research Council, 2014).

9. Pritchard, "How Do IRB Members Make Decisions?"

10. See National Research Council, *Proposed Revisions to the Common Rule*, 1–126.

11. See Stark, *Behind Closed Doors*, 229.

12. See Lederman, "The Perils of Working at Home"; Rena Lederman, "Educate Your IRB: An Experiment in Cross-Disciplinary Communication," *Anthropology News* 48 (2007): 33–34; Daniel Bradburd, "Fuzzy Boundaries and Hard Rules: Unfunded Research and the IRB," *American Ethnologist* 33, no. 4 (2006): 492–98; IRB Advisor, "Researcher Promotes IRB Efficiency Rating System," *IRB Advisor* (October 1, 2011); IRB Advisor, "Dealing with Ethnographic Issues," *IRB Advisor* (September 1, 2006).

13. According to the 1991 Common Rule, documentation of informed consent could be waived if "the only record linking the subject and the research would be the consent document and the principal risk would be potential harm resulting from a breach of confidentiality," *or* if "the research presents no more than minimal risk of harm to subjects and involves no procedures for which written consent is normally required outside of the research context." "Protection of Human Subjects," Code of Federal Regulations, Title 45, Part 46 (1991): sec. 117.

14. National Research Council, *Proposed Revisions to the Common Rule*, 95.

15. On buffering, see Thompson, *Organizations in Action*; on mimetic isomorphism, see DiMaggio and Powell, "The Iron Cage Revisited."

16. National Research Council, *Proposed Revisions to the Common Rule*, 94.

17. The office argued that they had not relaxed their vigilance and that they were choosing to address allegations of noncompliance through other mechanisms, such as contacting institutions directly. See Daniel R. Levison, *OHRP Generally Conducted Its Compliance Activities Independently, but Changes Would Strengthen Its Independence* (U.S. Department of Health and Human Services, Office of Inspector General, 2017), https://oig.hhs.gov/oei/reports/oei-01-15-00350.asp.

18. See IRB Advisor, "Take Steps Now to Reduce Burden," *IRB Advisor* (September 1, 2012).

19. The initiative was led by Associate Vice President for Research Judy Nowack, with the collaboration of two administrators with responsibilities within the University of Michigan's IRB system, Lois Brako and Judy Birk. I am indebted to Lois Brako for her description of how the initiative unfolded.

20. The coalition was the brainchild of Susan Rose, the executive director of the USC Office for the Protection of Research Subjects. See University of Southern California, Office for the Protection of Research Subjects, "Flexibility Coalition," https://oprs

.usc.edu/about/initiatives/flexibility-coalition/ (accessed December 19, 2017); National Research Council, *Proposed Revisions to the Common Rule*, 139.

21. University of Southern California, Office for the Protection of Research Subjects, "Flexibility Coalition"; National Research Council, *Proposed Revisions to the Common Rule*, 139.

22. Federal Demonstration Partnership, "Practical Guide for Reducing Regulatory Burden," National Academies of Sciences, Engineering, and Medicine, http://sites .nationalacademies.org/PGA/fdp/PGA_061067 (accessed December 18, 2017).

23. University of Southern California, Office for the Protection of Research Subjects, "Flexibility Coalition."

24. The "finding flexibility" track was featured at the organization's 2007 Social, Behavioral and Educational Research (SBER) miniconference. Regulators presented at the larger PRIM&R conference that year; Public Responsibility in Medicine and Research (PRIM&R), "Past Conferences," https://www.primr.org/conferences/past/ (accessed December 19, 2017).

25. Ibid.

26. Public Responsibility in Medicine and Research (PRIM&R), *Response to the Notice of Proposed Rulemaking*, 2015, https://www.regulations.gov/document?D=HHS -OPHS-2015-0008-1053.

27. Dobbin, *Inventing Equal Opportunity*; Edelman et al., "When Organizations Rule."

28. U.S. Department of Health and Human Services, *Human Subjects Research Protections*.

29. Ibid., p. 44513.

30. These included "scholarly and journalistic activities (e.g., oral history, journalism, biography, literary criticism, legal research, and historical scholarship), including the collection and use of information, that focus directly on the specific individuals about whom the information is collected." See "Protection of Human Subjects," Code of Federal Regulations, Title 45, Part 46 (2018): sec. 102.

31. Robert Dingwall, "Social Sciences Lose Out Again in Common Rule Reform," *Nature Human Behavior* 1, no. 4 (2017): 1; Schrag, "A Social Scientist's Guide to the Final Rule."

32. U.S. Department of Health and Human Services et al., "Federal Policy for the Protection of Human Subjects," *Federal Register* 82, no. 12 (2017): 7184.

33. See Richard A. Shweder and Richard E. Nisbett, "Don't Let Your Misunderstanding of the Rules Hinder Your Research," *Chronicle of Higher Education*, April 19, 2017, https://www.chronicle.com/article/Don-t-Let-Your/239823.

34. U.S. Department of Health of Human Services et al., *Federal Policy for the Protection of Human Subjects*, 7181.

35. Shweder and Nisbett, "Don't Let Your Misunderstanding of the Rules Hinder Your Research."

36. Ehrhardt, Appel, and Meinert, "Trends in National Institutes of Health Funding for Clinical Trials Registered in ClinicalTrials.gov."

Chapter 6: Varieties of Compliance

1. Lyndon B. Johnson, "Radio and Television Remarks upon Signing the Civil Rights Bill," July 2, 1964, The American Presidency Project, https://www.presidency.ucsb.edu/documents/radio-and-television-remarks-upon-signing-the-civil-rights-bill.

2. See Kalev, Dobbin, and Kelly, "Best Practices or Best Guesses?"; Edelman, "Legal Ambiguity and Symbolic Structures," 1542.

3. Ruthanne Huising and Susan S. Silbey, "Governing the Gap: Forging Safe Science through Relational Regulation," *Regulation & Governance* 5, no. 1 (2011): 14–42; Dobbin, *Inventing Equal Opportunity*; Brennan, "Constructing Risk and Legitimizing Place."

4. Dobbin, *Inventing Equal Opportunity*, 86; Edelman, "Legal Ambiguity and Symbolic Structures," 1542; Kalev, Dobbin, and Kelly, "Best Practices or Best Guesses?," 610.

5. Jeffrey Marshall and Ellen M. Heffes, "For CFOs, the To-Do List Lengthens," *Financial Executive*, November 2002, 26.

6. Federal sentencing guidelines explicitly allowed for the mitigation of penalties for a firm that had "an effective compliance program." See Donald C. Langevoort, "Internal Controls after Sarbanes-Oxley: Revisiting Corporate Law's Duty of Care as Responsibility for Systems," *Journal of Corporation Law* 31, no. 3 (2005): 949.

7. Securities Industry and Financial Markets Association, *The Evolving Role of Compliance*, March 2013, https://www.sifma.org/wp-content/uploads/2017/05/the-evolving-role-of-compliance.pdf.

8. Anthony Effinger, "The Rise of the Compliance Guru—and Banker Ire," *Bloomberg Markets*, June 25, 2015, https://www.bloomberg.com/news/features/2015-06-25/compliance-is-now-calling-the-shots-and-bankers-are-bristling.

9. Jaclyn Jaeger, "Salaries, Bonuses Rise for Banking Compliance Execs," *Compliance Week*, January 2014, 1, 37–39.

10. National Society of Compliance Professionals, "About NCSP," National Society of Compliance Professionals, https://nscp.org/about-cscp/ (accessed January 22, 2019).

11. Securities Industry and Financial Markets Association, *The Evolving Role of Compliance*.

12. Ibid.

13. Peter Farley, "Spotlight on Compliance Costs as Banks Get Down to Business with AI," *International Banker*, July 4, 2017, https://internationalbanker.com/technology/spotlight-compliance-costs-banks-get-business-ai/.

14. Paul R. Osborne, "Effective Compliance Management," *Community Banker* 16, no. 11 (2007): 62–64.

15. Loring Muir, quoted in John Ehrensperger, "Bank Compliance Officers' Top Priorities: Find New Ways to Control New Risks," *Bank Systems and Technology* (October 2003): 35.

16. Securities Industry and Financial Markets Association, *The Evolving Role of Compliance*.

17. Farley, "Spotlight on Compliance Costs."

18. Stacey English and Susannah Hammond, "Cost of Compliance Report 2017: Is There a New Risk Approach?," Thomson Reuters, https://blogs.thomsonreuters.com /financial-risk/risk-management-and-compliance/cost-of-compliance-report-2017-is -there-a-new-risk-approach/ (accessed July 7, 2018).

19. Mark Schoeff, "SEC Warns Advisers about Outsourcing Compliance," *Investment News*, November 9, 2015, http://www.investmentnews.com/article/20151109 /FREE/151109931/sec-warns-advisers-about-outsourcing-compliance;%20https://www .cio.com/article/3049474/outsourcing/is-outsourcing-it-worth-the-compliance-risk .html.

20. Julie Dimauro, "Impact Analysis: Managing the Risks of Compliance Outsourcing," Reuters, http://blogs.reuters.com/financial-regulatory-forum/2015/12/01/impact -analysis-managing-the-risks-of-compliance-outsourcing/ (accessed July 7, 2018).

21. Michael Power, "Making Things Auditable," *Accounting, Organizations and Society* 21, no. 2–3 (1996): 289–315.

22. John Meyer and Brian Rowan. "Institutionalized Organizations: Formal Structure as Myth and Ceremony," *American Journal of Sociology* 83, no. 2 (1977): 340–63.

23. Alexandra Kalev and Frank Dobbin, "Enforcement of Civil Rights Law in Private Workplaces: The Effects of Compliance Reviews and Lawsuits over Time," *Law and Social Inquiry* 31, no. 4 (2006): 855–903.

24. Linda Hamilton Krieger, Rachel Kahn Best, and Lauren B. Edelman, "When 'Best Practices' Win, Employees Lose: Symbolic Compliance and Judicial Inference in Federal Equal Employment Opportunity Cases," *Law & Social Inquiry* 40, no. 4 (2015): 843; Kalev, Dobbin, and Kelly, "Best Practices or Best Guesses?"; Edelman et al., "When Organizations Rule."

25. Braithwaite, "Enforced Self-Regulation"; Robyn Fairman and Charlotte Yapp, "Enforced Self-Regulation, Prescription, and Conceptions of Compliance within Small Businesses: The Impact of Enforcement," *Law & Policy* 27, no. 4 (2005): 491–519; Power, *The Audit Society*; Michael Power, "The Audit Society—Second Thoughts," *International Journal of Auditing* 4, no. 1 (2000): 111–19.

26. Michelle Jacko, "Regulatory Examinations and Audits," in *Modern Compliance: Best Practices for Securities and Finance*, ed. David H. Lui and John H. Walsh (New York: Wolters Kluwer Financial Services, 2015), 582.

27. Michael Power has noted the "hidden direct and indirect financial costs of audit compliance as organizations engage in elaborate strategies to make themselves auditable." Power, *The Audit Society*, 190.

28. Ehrensperger, "Bank Compliance Officers' Top Priorities."

29. Farley, "Spotlight on Compliance Costs."

30. Edelman, "Legal Ambiguity and Symbolic Structures," 1542.

31. The worlds of Title IX and EEO compliance overlap; they respond to different parts of the same law (EEO is most relevant to Titles VI and VII), and in universities are often administered by the same staff members.

32. R. S. Melnick, *The Transformation of Title IX: Regulating Gender Equality in Education* (Washington, DC: Brookings Institution Press, 2018).

33. Ibid. Recordkeeping requirements were heightened by the Violence against Women Act in 2013 requiring schools to engage in more extensive reporting on sexual violence and to document their prevention efforts. Ibid., 198.

34. Maxient "helps institutions manage student incident reports online by sending automated letters and forms, tracking student demographics and sending student and staff email and text alerts. The software records all things relative to conduct, including symbolic affairs, academic integrity, mediation and threat assessment." See Lauren Williams, "Higher Ed Leaders Select the Most Effective Products of the Year," *University Business*, January 2014, https://universitybusiness.com/higher-ed-leaders -select-the-most-effective-products-of-the-year/.

35. Melnick, *The Transformation of Title IX*, 203.

36. Power, *The Audit Society*.

37. Burris and Welsh, "Regulatory Paradox," 643; Halpern, "Hybrid Design, Systemic Rigidity"; Carol A. Heimer and JuLeigh Petty, "Bureaucratic Ethics: IRBs and the Legal Regulation of Human Subjects Research," *Annual Review of Law and Social Science* 6 (2010): 601–26.

38. Kalev and Dobbin, "Enforcement of Civil Rights Law."

Conclusion

1. Bioethicists had argued for much tougher restrictions, and the treatment of biospecimens in the final rule was characterized by *Inside Higher Ed* as a "major win for the associations that lobby on behalf of research universities," including the Association of American Universities and the Association of Public and Land-Grant Universities. Scott Jaschik, "New 'Common Rule' for Research," *Inside Higher Ed*, January 19, 2017.

2. James Miessler, "FDA Guidance Clarifies Agency Regulations v. Revised Common Rule," *CenterWatch Monthly*, October 2018, sec. 22.

3. Bruce Gordon, quoted in IRB Advisor [Melinda Young], "Beware of Good and Bad News about the New Common Rule," *IRB Advisor* (December 1, 2018).

4. Balogh, *The Associational State*; Clemens, "Lineages of the Rube Goldberg State," 189; Farhang, *The Litigation State*; Campbell and Morgan, *The Delegated Welfare State*.

5. National Bioethics Advisory Commission, "Ethical and Policy Issues in Research Involving Human Participants"; Koski, "Beyond Compliance."

6. Kaplan, "In Clinical Trials, For-Profit Review Boards Are Taking Over."

7. IRB Advisor, "OHRP Move Might Increase Trend of Research Sites Using Central IRBs," *IRB Advisor* (August 1, 2010).

8. IRB Advisor, "Preparation, Communication Key to Establishing IRB of Record," *IRB Advisor* (April 1, 2018).

9. Ropes & Gray, "21st Century Cures Act—Provisions Relating to Regulation of Clinical Research," Ropes & Gray, https://www.ropesgray.com/en/newsroom/alerts/2016/December/21st-Century-Cures-Act-Provisions-Relating-to-Regulation-of-Clinical-Research (accessed January 18, 2018).

10. "Proposed Rewrite of Human Research Protections Draws Resistance," *Congressional Quarterly News*, August 7, 2016.

11. IRB Advisor, "Preparation, Communication Key to Establishing IRB of Record."

12. Ibid.

13. Public Responsibility in Medicine and Research (PRIM&R), "Membership Data," unpublished internal database.

14. Joshua Hatch, "Why a Federal Rule Change Has Some Scholars Worried They'll Be Priced Out of Their Own Research," *Chronicle of Higher Education*, August 23, 2018, https://www.chronicle.com/article/Why-a-Federal-Rule-Change-Has/244344.

15. The comprehensive term often used for these diverse bodies (including IRBs in the United States) is "research ethics committees," or RECs. Fitzgerald and Phillips, "Centralized and Non-centralized Ethics Review"; Salman et al., "Increasing Value and Reducing Waste"; Nicholls et al., "Call for a Pan-Canadian Approach to Ethics Review in Canada.

16. See Hedgecoe et al., "Research Ethics Committees in Europe"; Jaspers, Houtepen, and Horstman, "Ethical Review"; Stoffel et al., *Ethics Assessment in Different Countries*.

17. K. G. Alberti, "Local Research Ethics Committees," *BMJ (Clinical Research Ed.)* 311, no. 7006 (1995): 639.

18. Hedgecoe et al., "Research Ethics Committees in Europe."

19. Salman et al., "Increasing Value and Reducing Waste."

20. United Kingdom Health Research Authority, "Central Booking Service," United Kingdom Health Research Authority, https://www.hra.nhs.uk/about-us/committees-and-services/central-booking-service/ (accessed January 17, 2019).

21. United Kingdom Health Research Authority, "Research Ethics Committee—Standard Operating Procedures," United Kingdom Health Research Authority, https://www.hra.nhs.uk/about-us/committees-and-services/res-and-recs/research-ethics-committee-standard-operating-procedures/ (accessed January 17, 2019).

22. Fitzgerald and Phillips, "Centralized and Non-centralized Ethics Review."

23. United Kingdom Health Research Authority, "Research Ethics Committee—Standard Operating Procedures."

24. U.S. Congress, House, Committee on Government Reform and Oversight, Subcommittee on Human Resources, *Institutional Review Boards*; U.S. General Accounting Office, *Scientific Research*; U.S. Department of Health and Human Services, Office of the Inspector General, *Protecting Human Research Subjects*; U.S. Department of Health and Human Services, Office of the Inspector General, *Institutional Review Boards*.

25. On the rulemaking process, see Thomas O. McGarity, "Some Thoughts on Deossifying the Rulemaking Process," *Duke Law Journal* 41 (1991): 1385; Richard J. Pierce Jr., "Rulemaking and the Administrative Procedure Act," *Tulsa Law Journal* 32 (1996): 185.

26. See Braithwaite, "Enforced Self-Regulation."

27. See Dobbin, *Inventing Equal Opportunity*; Campbell and Morgan, *The Delegated Welfare State*.

28. Babb, Birk, and Carfagna, "Standard Bearers."

29. In a 2014 report on revising the Common Rule, the National Research Council recommended that IRBs be required to have an appeals mechanism, but this did not make it into the final rule. National Research Council, *Proposed Revisions to the Common Rule*.

30. The base fee for continuing review was $1,166, plus $1,100 for each principal investigator. WIRB-Copernicus Group, "2018 Single Review Service Fee Schedule."

31. Kaplan, "In Clinical Trials, For-Profit Review Boards Are Taking Over."

32. However, FDA oversight has been more robust: the agency reports that during the 2017 fiscal year, it conducted 124 inspections. See https://www.fda.gov/downloads/ScienceResearch/SpecialTopics/RunningClinicalTrials/UCM604510.pdf.

33. Quote from presidential candidate Donald J. Trump, in Lisa Rein and Andrew Tran, "How the Trump Era Is Changing the Federal Bureaucracy," *Washington Post*, December 30, 2017.

34. These were Scott Gottlieb and Alex Azar, respectively. Azar took over the department following the scandal-ridden resignation of Tom Price.

Bibliography

Abbott, Laura, and Christine Grady. "A Systematic Review of the Empirical Literature Evaluating IRBs: What We Know and What We Still Need to Learn." *Journal of Empirical Research on Human Research Ethics* 6, no. 1 (2011): 3–20.

Alberti, K. G. "Local Research Ethics Committees." *British Medical Journal (Clinical Research Ed.)* 311, no. 7006 (1995): 639–40.

American Association of University Professors. "Research on Human Subjects: Academic Freedom and the Institutional Review Board." http://www.aaup.org/AAUP /comm/rep/A/humansubs.htm (accessed January 23, 2010).

Association for the Accreditation of Human Research Protection Programs (AAHRPP). *Accreditation for Human Research Protection Programs.* Washington, DC: AAHRPP, 2017.

———. "Accredited Organizations." http://www.aahrpp.org/learn/find-an-accredited -organization (accessed October 16, 2016).

———. "Application Fees 2017." https://admin.share.aahrpp.org/Website%20Docu ments/Application%20Fees%202017%20-%20Domestic.pdf (accessed November 16, 2017).

———. "Pfizer Is First Pharmaceutical Company to Earn Accreditation." http://www .aahrpp.org/apply/web-document-library/pfizer-is-first-pharmaceutical-company -to-earn-accreditation (accessed October 13, 2016).

Babb, Sarah, Lara Birk, and Luka Carfagna. "Standard Bearers: Qualitative Sociologists' Experiences with IRB Regulation." *American Sociologist* 48, no. 1 (2017): 86–102.

Babb, Sarah L. *Managing Mexico: Economists from Nationalism to Neoliberalism.* Princeton, NJ: Princeton University Press, 2001.

Bajpai, Kartikeya. "Cross-National Variation in Occupational Prestige." *Academy of Management Annual Meeting Proceedings* 2017, no. 1 (2017): 1.

Balogh, Brian. *The Associational State: American Governance in the Twentieth Century.* Philadelphia: University of Pennsylvania Press, 2015.

Basken, Paul. "Overhaul of Rules for Human Research Hits Impasse." *Chronicle of Higher Education,* March 22, 2013. https://www.chronicle.com/article/Overhaul -of-Rules-for-Human/137811.

Berman, Elizabeth Popp. *Creating the Market University: How Academic Science Became an Economic Engine.* Princeton, NJ: Princeton University Press, 2011.

Biomedical Research Alliance of New York (BRANY). "BRANY Announces Acquisition of University of Miami's CITI Program." http://www.brany.com/2016/05/13 /brany-announces-acquisition-university-miamis-citi-collaborative-institutional -training-initiative-program/ (accessed October 6, 2017).

Bledsoe, Caroline H., Bruce Sherin, Adam G. Galinsky, Nathalia M. Headley, Carol A. Heimer, Erik Kjeldgaard, James Lindgren, Jon D. Miller, Michael E. Roloff, and David H. Uttal. "Regulating Creativity: Research and Survival in the IRB Iron Cage." *Northwestern University Law Review* 101, no. 2 (2007): 593–641.

Blog de la Recherche Clinique. "Jarde Law in Practice." https://blogdelarechercheclinique .com/en/la-loi-jarde-en-pratique-le-cpp-et-lansm/ (accessed February 9, 2019).

Borror, Kristina, Michael Carome, Patrick McNeilly, and Carol Weil. "A Review of OHRP Compliance Oversight Letters." *IRB: Ethics and Human Research* 25, no. 5 (2003): 1–4.

Boyd, Elizabeth A. "Bureaucratic Authority in the Company of Equals: The Interactional Management of Medical Peer Review." *American Sociological Review* 63, no. 2 (1998): 200–224.

Bradburd, Daniel. "Fuzzy Boundaries and Hard Rules: Unfunded Research and the IRB." *American Ethnologist* 33, no. 4 (2006): 492–98.

Brainard, Jeffrey. "NIH, FDA Should Do More to Protect Human Subjects in Research, Report Says." *Chronicle of Higher Education,* April 21, 2000. https://www.chronicle .com/article/NIH-FDA-Should-Do-More-to/19529.

———. "Spate of Suspensions of Academic Research Spurs Questions about Federal Strategy: A U.S. Agency, Its Own Future Uncertain, Unsettles College Officials with Its Crackdown." *Chronicle of Higher Education,* February 4, 2000, A29–30, A32.

Braithwaite, John. "Enforced Self-Regulation: A New Strategy for Corporate Crime Control." *Michigan Law Review* 80, no. 7 (1982): 1466–507.

Braunschweiger, Paul, and Kenneth W. Goodman. "The CITI Program: An International Online Resource for Education in Human Subjects Protection and the Responsible Conduct of Research." *Academic Medicine* 82 (2007): 861–64.

Brennan, Elizabeth. "Constructing Risk and Legitimizing Place: Privacy Professionals' Interpretation and Implementation of HIPAA in Hospitals." Paper presented at the annual meetings of the American Sociological Association, Seattle, WA, August 2016.

Brown, DeNeen L. "'You've Got Bad Blood': The Horror of the Tuskegee Syphilis Experiment." *Washington Post*, May 16, 2017. https://www.washingtonpost.com /news/retropolis/wp/2017/05/16/youve-got-bad-blood-the-horror-of-the-tuskegee -syphilis-experiment/?utm_term=.2e00b1414b2f.

Burris, Scott, and Jen Welsh. "Regulatory Paradox: A Review of Enforcement Letters Issued by the Office for Human Research Protection." *Northwestern University Law Review* 101, no. 2 (2007): 643–85.

Campbell, Andrea Louise, and Kimberly J. Morgan. *The Delegated Welfare State: Medicare, Markets, and the Governance of Social Policy*. New York: Oxford University Press, 2011.

Carpenter, Daniel P. *Reputation and Power: Organizational Image and Pharmaceutical Regulation at the FDA*. Princeton, NJ: Princeton University Press, 2010.

Clemens, Elisabeth S. "Lineages of the Rube Goldberg State: Building and Blurring Public Programs, 1900–1940." In *Rethinking Political Institutions: The Art of the State*, edited by Stephen Skowronek and Daniel Galvin, 187–215. New York: New York University Press, 2006.

Collaborative Institutional Training Initiative (CITI). "Management Team." https:// about.citiprogram.org/en/leadership/ (accessed October 6, 2017).

———. "Mission and History." https://about.citiprogram.org/en/mission-and-history/ (accessed October 6, 2017).

———. "Organizational Subscriptions." https://about.citiprogram.org/en/orga nizational-subscriptions/ (accessed October 6, 2017).

Colyvas, Jeannette Anastasia. "From Divergent Meanings to Common Practices: Institutionalization Processes and the Commercialization of University Research." PhD diss., Stanford University, 2007.

DiMaggio, Paul J., and Walter W. Powell. "The Iron Cage Revisited: Institutional Isomorphism and Collective Rationality in Organizational Fields." *American Sociological Review* 48, no. 2 (April 1983): 147–60.

Dimauro, Julie. "Impact Analysis: Managing the Risks of Compliance Outsourcing." Reuters. http://blogs.reuters.com/financial-regulatory-forum/2015/12/01/impact -analysis-managing-the-risks-of-compliance-outsourcing/ (accessed July 7, 2018).

Dingwall, Robert. "Social Sciences Lose Out Again in Common Rule Reform." *Nature Human Behavior* 1, no. 4 (2017): 1.

Dobbin, Frank. *Inventing Equal Opportunity*. Princeton, NJ: Princeton University Press, 2009.

Dobbin, Frank, and John R. Sutton. "The Rights Revolution and the Rise of Human Resources Management Divisions." *American Journal of Sociology* 104, no. 2 (1998): 441–76.

Douglas-Jones, Rachel. "Getting Inside Ethical Review: Anxious Bureaucracies of Revelation, Anticipation and Virtue." *Critical Public Health* 29, no. 4 (2019): 448–59.

Edelman, Lauren B. "Legal Ambiguity and Symbolic Structures: Organizational Mediation of Civil Rights Law." *American Journal of Sociology* 97, no. 6 (1992): 1531–76.

Edelman, Lauren B., Linda H. Krieger, Scott R. Eliason, Catherine R. Albiston, and Virginia Mellema. "When Organizations Rule: Judicial Deference to Institutionalized Employment Structures." *American Journal of Sociology* 117, no. 3 (2011): 888–954.

Effinger, Anthony. "The Rise of the Compliance Guru—and Banker Ire." *Bloomberg Markets*, June 25, 2015. https://www.bloomberg.com/news/features/2015-06-25 /compliance-is-now-calling-the-shots-and-bankers-are-bristling.

Ehrensperger, John. "Bank Compliance Officers' Top Priorities: Find New Ways to Control New Risks." *Bank Systems and Technology* (October 2003).

Ehrhardt, Stephan, Lawrence J. Appel, and Curtis L. Meinert. "Trends in National Institutes of Health Funding for Clinical Trials Registered in ClinicalTrials.Gov." *JAMA* 314, no. 23 (2015): 2566–67.

English, Stacey, and Hammond, Susannah. "Cost of Compliance Report 2017: Is There a New Risk Approach?" Thomson Reuters, https://blogs.thomsonreuters.com /financial-risk/risk-management-and-compliance/cost-of-compliance-report -2017-is-there-a-new-risk-approach/ (accessed July 7, 2018).

Epstein, Melissa A., and Stephen Lascher. "Human Research Protection Programs." In *Implementing a Comprehensive Research Compliance Program: A Handbook for Research Officers*, edited by Aurali Dade, Lori Olafson, and Suzan M. DiBella, 10–26. Charlotte, NC: Information Age, 2016.

Fairman, Robyn, and Charlotte Yapp. "Enforced Self-Regulation, Prescription, and Conceptions of Compliance within Small Businesses: The Impact of Enforcement." *Law & Policy* 27, no. 4 (2005): 491–519.

Farhang, Sean. *The Litigation State: Public Regulation and Private Lawsuits in the United States*. Princeton, NJ: Princeton University Press, 2010.

Farley, Peter. "Spotlight on Compliance Costs as Banks Get Down to Business with AI." *International Banker*, July 4, 2017. https://internationalbanker.com/technology /spotlight-compliance-costs-banks-get-business-ai/.

Fassbender, Melissa. "IRB Consolidation Continues as Chesapeake and Schulman Merge to Form Advarra." *Outsourcing-Pharma.Com*, November 8, 2017. https://www.outsourcing-pharma.com/Article/2017/11/08/Chesapeake-IRB-and -Schulman-IRB-merge-to-form-Advarra.

Federal Demonstration Partnership. "Practical Guide for Reducing Regulatory Burden." National Academies of Sciences, Engineering, and Medicine. http://sites
.nationalacademies.org/PGA/fdp/PGA_061067 (accessed December 18, 2017).

Federation of American Societies for Experimental Biology. "NIH Research Funding Trends." http://faseb.org/Science-Policy--Advocacy-and-Communications
/Federal-Funding-Data/NIH-Research-Funding-Trends.aspx (accessed November 14, 2017).

Feeley, Malcolm M. "Legality, Social Research, and the Challenge of Institutional
Review Boards." *Law & Society Review* 41, no. 4 (2007): 757–76.

Fisher, Jill. *Medical Research for Hire: The Political Economy of Pharmaceutical Clinical
Trials*. New Brunswick, NJ: Rutgers University Press, 2008.

Fitzgerald, Maureen H. "Punctuated Equilibrium, Moral Panics and the Ethics Review
Process." *Journal of Academic Ethics* 2 (2004): 315–38.

Fitzgerald, Maureen H., and Paul A. Phillips. "Centralized and Non-centralized Ethics
Review: A Five Nation Study." *Accountability in Research* 13, no. 1 (2006): 47–74.

Frankel, Mark Steven. "Public Policymaking for Biomedical Research: The Case of
Human Experimentation." PhD diss., George Washington University, 1976.

Gawande, Atul. *The Checklist Manifesto: How to Get Things Right*. New York: Picador,
2011.

Gorman, Elizabeth H., and Rebecca L. Sandefur. "'Golden Age,' Quiescence, and Revival: How the Sociology of Professions Became the Study of Knowledge-Based
Work." *Work and Occupations* 38, no. 3 (2011): 275–302.

Green, Lawrence W. "From Research to 'Best Practices' in Other Settings and Populations." *American Journal of Health Behavior* 25, no. 3 (2001): 165–78.

Greenberg, Daniel S. *Science for Sale: The Perils, Rewards, and Delusions of Campus
Capitalism*. Chicago: University of Chicago Press, 2007.

Gunsalus, C. K., Edward M. Brunet, Nicholas C. Burbules, Leon Dash, Matthew
Finkin, Joseph P. Goldberg, William T. Greenough, Gregory A. Miller, and Michael G. Pratt. "Mission Creep in the IRB World." *Science* 312, no. 5779 (2006): 1441.

Haddock, Beth. *Triple Bottom-Line Compliance: How to Deliver Protection, Productiv-
ity, and Impact*. Charleston, SC: Advantage Media Group, 2018.

Hallett, Tim. "The Myth Incarnate: Recoupling Processes, Turmoil, and Inhabited
Institutions in an Urban Elementary School." *American Sociological Review* 75,
no. 1 (2010): 52–74.

Halpern, Sydney. "Hybrid Design, Systemic Rigidity: Institutional Dynamics in
Human Research Oversight." *Regulation & Governance* 2, no. 1 (2008): 85–102.

Hatch, Joshua. "Why a Federal Rule Change Has Some Scholars Worried They'll Be
Priced Out of Their Own Research." *Chronicle of Higher Education*, August 23, 2018.
https://www.chronicle.com/article/Why-a-Federal-Rule-Change-Has/244344.

Heath, Erica. *The History, Function, and Future of Independent Institutional Review Boards*. Washington, DC: Online Ethics Center, 2000. http://www.onlineethics.org/cms/8080.aspx.

Hedgecoe, A., F. Carvalho, P. Lobmayer, and F. Raka. "Research Ethics Committees in Europe: Implementing the Directive, Respecting Diversity." *Journal of Medical Ethics* 32, no. 8 (August 2006): 483–86.

Heimer, Carol A., and JuLeigh Petty. "Bureaucratic Ethics: IRBs and the Legal Regulation of Human Subjects Research." *Annual Review of Law and Social Science* 6 (2010): 601–26.

Heinrich, Janet. *Human Subjects Research: HHS Takes Steps to Strengthen Protections, but Concerns Remain*. Washington, DC: U.S. General Accounting Office, 2001.

Hilts, Philip J. "Agency Faults a U.C.L.A. Study for Suffering of Mental Patients." *New York Times*, March 10, 1994.

Hirsh, C. Elizabeth. "The Strength of Weak Enforcement: The Impact of Discrimination Charges, Legal Environments, and Organizational Conditions on Workplace Segregation." *American Sociological Review* 74, no. 2 (2009): 245–71.

Hoffman, Sharona, and Jessica Wilen Berg. "The Suitability of IRB Liability." *University of Pittsburgh Law Review* 67 (2005): 365–427.

Huising, Ruthanne, and Susan S. Silbey. "From Nudge to Culture and Back Again: Coalface Governance in the Regulated Organization." *Annual Review of Law and Social Science* 14 (2018): 91–114.

———. "Governing the Gap: Forging Safe Science through Relational Regulation." *Regulation & Governance* 5, no. 1 (2011): 14–42.

Huron Consulting Group. "IRB Transformation Solutions." https://www.huronconsultinggroup.com/-/media/Resource-Media-Content/Education/RES_IRB-Transformation-Sell-Sheet.pdf?la=en (accessed October 22, 2016).

iMedris. "IRB Software Overview." iMedris. https://imedris.com/Modules/IRB-Software (accessed July 7, 2018).

Institute of Medicine. *Preserving Public Trust: Accreditation and Human Research Participant Protection Programs*. Washington, DC: Institute of Medicine, 2001.

IRB Advisor. "Accreditation Expert Offers Assessment Tips." *IRB Advisor* (May 1, 2014).

———. "Accreditation Is Not for the Faint of Heart." *IRB Advisor* (September 1, 2003).

———. "Achieving Accreditation through Tough Times." *IRB Advisor* (October 1, 2013).

———. "Add Some Climbs and Hills to Typically Flat Career Path." *IRB Advisor* (July 14, 2016).

———. "Baylor Uses Its BRAAN to Improve IRB Operations." *IRB Advisor* (April 1, 2003).

——— [Melinda Young]. "Beware of Good and Bad News about the New Common Rule." *IRB Advisor* (December 1, 2018).

———. "Central IRBs: Consistency Increases, but So Does Confusion." *IRB Advisor* (October 1, 2014).

———. "The Changing World of Independent IRBs." *IRB Advisor* (October 1, 2014).

———. "CIP Certification Is Taking Off among IRB Staff." *IRB Advisor* (July 1, 2006).

———. "Data Driven: Accreditation Group Releases Metrics for IRB Performance." *IRB Advisor* (September 1, 2010).

———. "Dealing with Ethnographic Issues." *IRB Advisor* (September 1, 2006).

———. "Every Improvement Helps IRB Efficiencies." *IRB Advisor* (June 1, 2014).

———. "Expert Outlines Main Struggles, Solutions to Better Informed Consent." *IRB Advisor* (September 1, 2009).

———. "Experts: NIRB and IRB Share Are Alternatives to Central IRBs." *IRB Advisor* (July 1, 2015).

———. "Fairness and Common Sense Can Ease Tensions." *IRB Advisor* (August 1, 2006).

———. "Historians, OHRP and IRBs Looking for Common Ground on Oral History Projects." *IRB Advisor* (March 1, 2006).

———. "IC under Revised Common Rule Is Transparent, Tightened." *IRB Advisor* (November 1, 2015).

———. "Improve IRB Staffing Issues Following This Good Example." *IRB Advisor* (April 1, 2011).

———. "Institution's QI Form Serves as Educational Tool for PIs." *IRB Advisor* (November 1, 2007).

———. "IRB Certification Becomes Industry Gold Standard." *IRB Advisor* (October 1, 2010).

———. "IRB Costs Are Greater than Previous Estimates." *IRB Advisor* (July 1, 2005).

———. "IRB Cuts 35 Days from Protocol Turnaround." *IRB Advisor* (November 1, 2009).

———. "IRB Expert Strategies for Improving PI-IRB Relations." *IRB Advisor* (October 1, 2013).

———. "IRB Seals Fate by Approving Fake Protocol in Federal Sting." *IRB Advisor* (July 1, 2009).

———. "IRBs Tie Up Study with Informed Consent Changes." *IRB Advisor* (August 1, 2009).

———. "Making the Case for a New Electronic System." *IRB Advisor* (November 1, 2010).

———. "Managers of IRBs Can Save Time with Tech." *IRB Advisor* (October 1, 2010).

———. "Mission Creep: Is It Leading IRBs Astray?" *IRB Advisor* (April 1, 2006).

———. "NCI's Central IRB Saves Time, Money." *IRB Advisor* (February 1, 2010).

———. "New AAHRPP Metrics Show Less IRB Funding." *IRB Advisor* (September 1, 2011).

———. "OHRP Move Might Increase Trend of Research Sites Using Central IRBs." *IRB Advisor* (August 1, 2010).

———. "Preparation, Communication Key to Establishing IRB of Record." *IRB Advisor* (April 1, 2018).

———. "Protocols Involving Oral History Still Need Review." *IRB Advisor* (February 1, 2004).

———. "Reduce Complaints with New Policies and Procedures." *IRB Advisor* (April 1, 2007).

———. "Reporting Rules for Adverse Events, Unanticipated Problems Differ Slightly." *IRB Advisor* (March 1, 2004).

———. "Researcher Promotes IRB Efficiency Rating System." *IRB Advisor* (October 1, 2011).

———. "Should Administrators Be Voting Members?" *IRB Advisor* (July 1, 2005).

———. "Single IRB NIH Guidance May Leave More Questions than Answers." *IRB Advisor* (March 1, 2015).

———. "Special Report: Regulations and Rules—Are we Heading in the Right Direction?" *IRB Advisor* (July 1, 2004).

———. "Spotlight on Compliance: Is Data Collection Research? It Depends: OHRP Clarifies Use of Data in Research." *IRB Advisor* (October 1, 2004).

———. "Staffing, Collaborations Top IRB Issues." *IRB Advisor* (January 1, 2014).

———. "Supply and Demand: IRB Fees Now Are the Norm." *IRB Advisor* (October 1, 2003).

———. "Take Steps Now to Reduce Burden." *IRB Advisor* (September 1, 2012).

———. "Teaching IRBs to Be Flexible, Drop Bad Habits." *IRB Advisor* (June 1, 2011).

———. "True Simplicity Remains Elusive for IC Forms." *IRB Advisor* (February 1, 2013).

———. "2003 Salary Survey Results." *IRB Advisor* (November 1, 2003).

———. "2008 Salary Survey Results: Economic Woes May Mean Less Hiring, Smaller Raises for IRB Professionals." *IRB Advisor* (January 1, 2009).

———. "With State University Budget Cuts It Might Be Time to Cut IRB Costs." *IRB Advisor* (April 1, 2009).

Irvine, Janice. "Can't Ask, Can't Tell: How Institutional Review Boards Keep Sex in the Closet." *Contexts* 11 (2012): 28–33.

Jacko, Michelle. "Regulatory Examinations and Audits." In *Modern Compliance: Best Practices for Securities and Finance*, edited by David H. Lui and John H. Walsh, 469–542. New York: Wolters Kluwer Financial Services, 2015.

Jaeger, Jaclyn. "Salaries, Bonus Rise for Banking Compliance Execs." *Compliance Week* (January 2014): 1, 37–39.

Jaschik, Scott. "New 'Common Rule' for Research." *Inside Higher Ed*, January 19, 2017.

Jaspers, Patricia, Rob Houtepen, and Klasien Horstman. "Ethical Review: Standard-izing Procedures and Local Shaping of Ethical Review Practices." *Social Science & Medicine* 98 (2013): 311–18.

Johnson, Lyndon B. "Radio and Television Remarks upon Signing the Civil Rights Bill," July 2, 1964. The American Presidency Project. https://www.presidency.ucsb.edu /documents/radio-and-television-remarks-upon-signing-the-civil-rights-bill.

Johnson, Tara Star. "Qualitative Research in Question: A Narrative of Disciplinary Power with/in the IRB." *Qualitative Inquiry* 14, no. 2 (2008): 212–32.

Kalev, Alexandra, and Frank Dobbin. "Enforcement of Civil Rights Law in Private Workplaces: The Effects of Compliance Reviews and Lawsuits over Time." *Law & Social Inquiry* 31, no. 4 (2006): 855–903.

Kalev, Alexandra, Frank Dobbin, and Erin Kelly. "Best Practices or Best Guesses? Assessing the Efficacy of Corporate Affirmative Action and Diversity Policies." *American Sociological Review* 71, no. 4 (2006): 589–617.

Kaplan, Sheila. "In Clinical Trials, For-Profit Review Boards Are Taking Over for Hospitals. Should They?" *STAT News*, July 6, 2016.

Katz, Jack. "Toward a Natural History of Ethical Censorship." *Law & Society Review* 41, no. 4 (December 2007): 797–810.

Klitzman, Robert. *The Ethics Police? The Struggle to Make Human Research Safe*. Oxford: Oxford University Press, 2015.

Korieth, Karyn. "AMCs Show Renewed Interest in Industry Research: New Collabo-rations, Greater Trust Breaking Down Research Silos." *CenterWatch Monthly*, November 2013, sec. 20.

Koski, Greg. "Beyond Compliance . . . Is It Too Much to Ask?" *IRB: Ethics & Human Research* 25, no. 5 (2002): 5–6.

Krieger, Linda Hamilton, Rachel Kahn Best, and Lauren B. Edelman. "When 'Best Practices' Win, Employees Lose: Symbolic Compliance and Judicial Inference in Federal Equal Employment Opportunity Cases." *Law & Social Inquiry* 40, no. 4 (2015): 843–79.

Landers, Steven H., and Ashwini R. Sehgal. "Health Care Lobbying in the United States." *American Journal of Medicine* 116, no. 7 (2004): 474–77.

Langevoort, Donald C. "Internal Controls after Sarbanes-Oxley: Revisiting Corporate Law's Duty of Care as Responsibility for Systems." *Journal of Corporation Law* 31, no. 3 (2006): 949–73.

Lederman, Rena. "Educate Your IRB: An Experiment in Cross-Disciplinary Com-munication." *Anthropology News* 48 (2007): 33–34.

———. "The Perils of Working at Home: IRB 'Mission Creep' as Context and Content for an Ethnography of Disciplinary Knowledges." *American Ethnologist* 33, no. 4 (2006): 482–91.

Leidner, Robin. *Fast Food, Fast Talk: Service Labor and the Routinization of Everyday Life*. Berkeley: University of California Press, 1993.

Levison, Daniel R. *OHRP Generally Conducted Its Compliance Activities Independently, but Changes Would Strengthen Its Independence*. Washington, DC: U.S. Department of Health and Human Services, Office of Inspector General, 2017. https://oig .hhs.gov/oei/reports/oei-01-15-00350.asp.

Loe, Jonathan D., D. Alex Winkelman, and Christopher T. Robertson. "An Assessment of the Human Subjects Protection Review Process for Exempt Research." *Journal of Law, Medicine & Ethics* 44, no. 3 (2016): 481–91.

Marshall, Jeffrey, and Ellen M. Heffes. "For CFOs, the To-Do List Lengthens." *Financial Executive*, November 2002, 26–31.

McCarthy, Charles R. "The Origins and Policies That Govern Institutional Review Boards." In *The Oxford Textbook of Clinical Research Ethics*, edited by Ezekiel J. Emmanuel, Christine Grady, Robert Crouch, Reidar K. Lie, Franklin G. Miller, and David Wendler, 50–75. New York: Oxford University Press, 2008.

———. "Reflections on the Organizational Locus of the Office for Protection from Research Risks." In *Ethical and Policy Issues in Research Involving Human Participants*, vol. 2, edited by National Bioethics Advisory Commission. Bethesda, MD: National Bioethics Advisory Commission, 2001. http://www.onlineethics .org/cms/17252.aspx.

McGarity, Thomas O. "Some Thoughts on Deossifying the Rulemaking Process." *Duke Law Journal* 41 (1992): 1385–1462.

McLaughlin, Curtis P., and Arnold D. Kaluzny. *Continuous Quality Improvement in Health Care: Theory, Implementation, and Applications*. Sudbury, MA: Jones & Bartlett Learning, 2004.

Medvetz, Thomas. *Think Tanks in America*. Chicago: University of Chicago Press, 2012.

Melnick, R. S. *The Transformation of Title IX: Regulating Gender Equality in Education*. Washington, DC: Brookings Institution Press, 2018.

Melnick, R. Shep. "From Tax and Spend to Mandate and Sue: Liberalism after the Great Society." In *The Great Society and the High Tide of Liberalism*, edited by Sidney M. Milkis and Jerome M. Mileur, 387–410. Amherst: University of Massachusetts Press, 2005.

Meyer, John W., and Brian Rowan. "Institutionalized Organizations: Formal Structure as Myth and Ceremony." *American Journal of Sociology* 83, no. 2 (1977): 340–63.

Michels, Robert. *Political Parties: A Sociological Study of the Oligarchical Tendencies of Modern Democracy*. New York: Dover Publications, 1959.

Miessler, James. "FDA Guidance Clarifies Agency Regulations v. Revised Common Rule." *CenterWatch Monthly*, October 2018, sec. 22.

Mirowski, Philip, and Robert Van Horn. "The Contract Research Organization and the Commercialization of Scientific Research." *Social Studies of Science* 35, no. 4 (2005): 503–48.

Moore, Colin D. "State Building through Partnership: Delegation, Public-Private Partnerships, and the Political Development of American Imperialism, 1898–1916." *Studies in American Political Development* 25, no. 1 (2011): 27–55.

Morgan, Kimberly J., and Andrea Louise Campbell. "Delegated Governance in the Affordable Care Act." *Journal of Health Politics, Policy and Law* 36, no. 3 (2011): 387–91.

National Bioethics Advisory Commission. *Ethical and Policy Issues in Research Involving Human Participants*. Vol. 1. Edited by National Bioethics Advisory Commission. Bethesda, MD: National Bioethics Advisory Commission, 2001. https://www.onlineethics.org/cms/8014.aspx.

National Institutes of Health. "NIH Almanac." National Institutes of Health. https://www.nih.gov/about-nih/what-we-do/nih-almanac/appropriations-section-2 (accessed July 5, 2016).

National Research Council. *Proposed Revisions to the Common Rule for the Protection of Human Subjects in the Behavioral and Social Sciences*. Washington, DC: National Research Council, 2014.

National Society of Compliance Professionals. "About NCSP." National Society of Compliance Professionals. https://nscp.org/about-cscp/ (accessed January 22, 2019).

Nicholls, Stuart G., Karine Morin, Laurel Evans, and Holly Longstaff. "Call for a Pan-Canadian Approach to Ethics Review in Canada." *Canadian Medical Association Journal* 190, no. 18 (2018): E553–55.

Nightingale, Stuart L. "Regulatory Overview: Protection of Human Subjects—IRBs and Informed Consent." *Drug Information Journal* 21, no. 2 (April 1, 1987): 109–15.

Northwestern University, Office for Research. "SOP Daily Tasks." https://irb.northwestern.edu/sites/irb/files/documents/hrp-062-sop-daily-tasks.pdf (accessed October 20, 2017).

Novak, William J. "The Myth of the 'Weak' American State." *American Historical Review* 113, no. 3 (2008): 752–72.

Office for Human Research Protections (OHRP). "FWAs." https://ohrp.cit.nih.gov/search/fwasearch.aspx?styp=bsc (accessed November 16, 2017).

———. "OHRP Determination Letters." https://www.hhs.gov/ohrp/compliance-and-reporting/determination-letters/index.html (accessed December 19, 2017).

———. "OHRP's Compliance Oversight Procedures for Evaluating Institutions." http://www.hhs.gov/ohrp/compliance-and-reporting/evaluating-institutions/ (accessed October 13, 2016).

Osborne, Paul R. "Effective Compliance Management." *Community Banker* 16, no. 11 (2007): 62–64.

Pedriana, Nicholas, and Robin Stryker. "The Strength of a Weak Agency: Enforce-
    ment of Title VII of the 1964 Civil Rights Act and the Expansion of State Capacity,
    1965–1971." *American Journal of Sociology* 110, no. 3 (2004): 709–60.
Pernell, Kim, Jiwook Jung, and Frank Dobbin. "The Hazards of Expert Control: Chief
    Risk Officers and Risky Derivatives." *American Sociological Review* 82, no. 3 (2017):
    511–41.
Pharmaceutical Research and Manufacturers of America (PhRMA). Home Page.
    http://www.phrma.org/ (accessed June 30, 2017).
Pierce, Richard J., Jr. "Rulemaking and the Administrative Procedure Act." *Tulsa Law
    Journal* 32 (1996): 185–201.
Plattner, Stuart. "Human Subjects Protection and Cultural Anthropology." *Anthropo-
    logical Quarterly* 76, no. 2 (2003): 287–97.
Porter, J., and Greg Koski. "Regulations for the Protection of Humans in Research in
    the United States." In *The Oxford Textbook of Clinical Research Ethics*, edited by
    Ezekiel J. Emmanuel, Christine Grady, Robert Crouch, Reidar K. Lie, Franklin G.
    Miller, and David Wendler, 156–67. New York: Oxford University Press, 2008.
Power, Michael. *The Audit Society: Rituals of Verification*. New York: Oxford University
    Press, 1997.
———. "The Audit Society—Second Thoughts." *International Journal of Auditing* 4,
    no. 1 (2000): 111–19.
———. "Making Things Auditable." *Accounting, Organizations and Society* 21, no. 2–3
    (1996): 289–315.
Prentice, Ernest, Sally L. Mann, and Bruce G. Gordon. "Charging for Institutional
    Review Board Review." In *Institutional Review Board: Management and Function*,
    edited by Elizabeth A. Bankert, Robert J. Amdur, chap. 2. 2nd ed. Boston: Jones
    and Bartlett, 2006.
Price, Byron E., and Norma M. Riccucci. "Exploring the Determinants of Decisions
    to Privatize State Prisons." *American Review of Public Administration* 35, no. 3
    (2005): 223–35.
PricewaterhouseCoopers. Promotional flyer for *The IRB Reference Book*. http://www
    .proirb.com/files/IRB%20Ref.Book%20Flyer3-11.16.01.pdf (accessed October 6,
    2017).
Pritchard, Ivor. "How Do IRB Members Make Decisions? A Review and Research
    Agenda." *Journal of Empirical Research on Human Research Ethics* 6 (2011): 31–46.
"Proposed Rewrite of Human Research Protections Draws Resistance." *Congressional
    Quarterly News*, August 7, 2016.
"Protection of Human Subjects." Code of Federal Regulations, Title 45, Part 46 (1974).
"Protection of Human Subjects." Code of Federal Regulations, Title 45, Part 46 (1981).
"Protection of Human Subjects." Code of Federal Regulations, Title 45, Part 46 (1991).

"Protection of Human Subjects." Code of Federal Regulations, Title 45, Part 46 (2018).

Public Responsibility in Medicine and Research (PRIM&R). "History." http://www.primr.org/about/history/ (accessed October 14, 2016).

———. "Membership Data." Unpublished internal database. 2019.

———. "Past Conferences." https://www.primr.org/conferences/past/ (accessed December 19, 2017).

———. *Program: 2017 Advancing Ethical Research Conference.* Boston: PRIM&R, 2017.

———. *Response to the Notice of Proposed Rulemaking.* 2015. https://www.regulations.gov/document?D=HHS-OPHS-2015-0008-1053.

———. "Workload and Salary Survey, 2007." https://www.primr.org/wlss/ (accessed June 29, 2017).

Quinn, Sarah Lehman. "Government Policy, Housing, and the Origins of Securitization, 1780–1968." PhD diss., University of California, Berkeley, 2010.

Rein, Lisa, and Andrew Tran. "How the Trump Era Is Changing the Federal Bureaucracy." *Washington Post*, December 30, 2017.

Rettig, Richard A. "The Industrialization of Clinical Research." *Health Affairs* 19, no. 2 (March–April 2000): 129–46.

Rockwell, Sara. "The FDP Faculty Burden Survey." *Research Management Review* 16, no. 2 (Spring 2009): 29–44.

Ropes & Gray. "21st Century Cures Act—Provisions relating to Regulation of Clinical Research." Ropes & Gray. https://www.ropesgray.com/en/newsroom/alerts/2016/December/21st-Century-Cures-Act-Provisions-Relating-to-Regulation-of-Clinical-Research (accessed January 18, 2018).

Rosenberg, Ronald. "AMCs Vying to Better Compete for Industry Trials: Working to Conquer Study Start-Up Delays, IRB Review Process." *CenterWatch Monthly*, December 2014, sec. 21.

Rosenthal, Elisabeth. "New York Seeks to Tighten Rules on Medical Research." *New York Times*, September 27, 1996.

Salman, Rustam Al-Shahi, Elaine Beller, Jonathan Kagan, Elina Hemminki, Robert S. Phillips, Julian Savulescu, Malcolm Macleod, Janet Wisely, and Iain Chalmers. "Increasing Value and Reducing Waste in Biomedical Research Regulation and Management." *The Lancet* 383, no. 9912 (2014): 176–85.

Schneider, Carl. *The Censor's Hand: The Misregulation of Human-Subject Research.* New York: New York University Press, 2015.

Schoeff, Mark. "SEC Warns Advisers about Outsourcing Compliance." *Investment News*, November 9, 2015. http://www.investmentnews.com/article/20151109/FREE/151109931/sec-warns-advisers-about-outsourcing-compliance;%20https://www.cio.com/article/3049474/outsourcing/is-outsourcing-it-worth-the-compliance-risk.html.

Schrag, Zachary M. *Ethical Imperialism: Institutional Review Boards and the Social Sciences, 1965–2009*. Baltimore: Johns Hopkins University Press, 2010.

———. "A Social Scientist's Guide to the Final Rule." *Institutional Review Blog*, January 19, 2017. http://www.institutionalreviewblog.com/2017/01/a-social-scientists -guide-to-final-rule.html.

Scott, W. Richard, Martin Ruef, Peter Mendel, and Carol Caronna. *Institutional Change and Healthcare Organizations: From Professional Dominance to Managed Care*. Chicago: University of Chicago Press, 2000.

Securities Industry and Financial Markets Association. *The Evolving Role of Compliance*. March 2013. https://www.sifma.org/wp-content/uploads/2017/05/the -evolving-role-of-compliance.pdf.

Shalala, Donna. "Protecting Research Subjects—What Must Be Done." *New England Journal of Medicine* 343, no. 11 (2000): 808–10.

Shweder, Richard A., and Richard E. Nisbett. "Don't Let Your Misunderstanding of the Rules Hinder Your Research." *Chronicle of Higher Education*, April 19, 2017. https://www.chronicle.com/article/Don-t-Let-Your/239823.

Silverman, Henry, Sara Chandros Hull, and Jeremy Sugarman. "Variability among Institutional Review Boards' Decisions within the Context of a Multicenter Trial." *Critical Care Medicine* 29, no. 2 (2001): 235–41.

Speckman, Jeanne L., Margaret M. Byrne, Jason Gerson, Kenneth Getz, Gary Wangsmo, Carianne T. Muse, and Jeremy Sugarman. "Determining the Costs of Institutional Review Boards." *IRB: Ethics & Human Research* 29, no. 2 (2007): 7–13.

Stair, Thomas O., Caitlin R. Reed, Michael S. Radeos, Greg Koski, and Carlos A. Camargo. "Variation in Institutional Review Board Responses to a Standard Protocol for a Multicenter Clinical Trial." *Academic Emergency Medicine* 8, no. 6 (2001): 636–41.

Stark, Laura Jeanine Morris. *Behind Closed Doors: IRBs and the Making of Ethical Research*. Chicago: University of Chicago Press, 2012.

Starr, Paul, 1949. *Remedy and Reaction: The Peculiar American Struggle over Health Care Reform*. New Haven, CT: Yale University Press, 2011.

Stoffel, Delphine, Ingrid Callies, Katrine Rojkova, and Sudeep Rangi. *Ethics Assessment in Different Countries: France*. European Commission, 2015. http://satoriproject .eu/media/4.d-Country-report-France.pdf.

Stolberg, Sheryl Gay. "Teenager's Death Is Shaking Up Field of Human Gene-Therapy Experiments." *New York Times*, January 27, 2001.

Thompson, James D. *Organizations in Action*. New York: McGraw-Hill, 1967.

Tierney, William G., and Zoe Blumberg Corwin. "The Tensions between Academic Freedom and Institutional Review Boards." *Qualitative Inquiry* 13, no. 3 (2007): 388–98.

United Kingdom Health Research Authority. "Central Booking Service." United King-
    dom Health Research Authority. https://www.hra.nhs.uk/about-us/committees
    -and-services/central-booking-service/ (accessed January 17, 2019).
———. "Research Ethics Committee—Standard Operating Procedures." United King-
    dom Health Research Authority. https://www.hra.nhs.uk/about-us/committees
    -and-services/res-and-recs/research-ethics-committee-standard-operating
    -procedures/ (accessed January 17, 2019).
University of Southern California. Office for the Protection of Research Subjects.
    "Flexibility Coalition." https://oprs.usc.edu/about/initiatives/flexibility-coalition/
    (accessed December 19, 2017).
U.S. Congress. House. Committee on Government Reform and Oversight. Subcom-
    mittee on Human Resources. *Institutional Review Boards, a System in Jeopardy:
    Hearing before the Subcommittee on Human Resources of the Committee on Govern-
    ment Reform and Oversight, House of Representatives, One Hundred Fifth Congress,
    Second Session, June 11, 1998.* Washington, DC: Government Printing Office, 1999.
U.S. Congress. House. Committee on Interstate and Foreign Commerce. *Biomedical
    Research Ethics and the Protection of Human Research Subjects: Hearings before
    the Subcommittee on Public Health and Environment of the Committee on Inter-
    state and Foreign Commerce, House of Representatives, Ninety-Third Congress, First
    Session . . . September 27 and 28, 1973.* Washington, DC: Government Printing
    Office, 1974.
U.S. Congress. House. Committee on Small Business. Subcommittee on Regulation,
    Business Opportunities, and Technology. *Problems in Securing Informed Consent
    of Subjects in Experimental Trials of Unapproved Drugs and Devices: Hearing be-
    fore the Subcommittee on Regulation, Business Opportunities, and Technology of
    the Committee on Small Business, House of Representatives, One Hundred Third
    Congress, Second Session, Washington, DC, May 23, 1994.* Washington, DC: Gov-
    ernment Printing Office, 1994.
U.S. Congress. Senate. Committee on Health, Education, Labor, and Pensions. Sub-
    committee on Public Health. *Protecting Human Subjects in Research: Are Current
    Safeguards Adequate? Hearing before the Subcommittee on Public Health of the Com-
    mittee on Health, Education, Labor, and Pensions, United States Senate, One Hun-
    dred Seventh Congress, Second Session, on Examining Current Safeguards concerning
    the Protection of Human Subjects in Research, while Facilitating Critical Medical
    Research, April 23, 2002.* Washington, DC: Government Printing Office, 2002.
U.S. Congress. Senate. Committee on Labor and Public Welfare. Subcommittee on
    Health. *Quality of Health Care—Human Experimentation, 1973. Hearings, Ninety-
    Third Congress, First Session, on S. 974.* Washington, DC: Government Printing
    Office, 1973.

U.S. Department of Health and Human Services. *Human Subjects Research Protec-tions: Enhancing Protections for Research Subjects and Reducing Burden, Delay, and Ambiguity for Investigators (Advance Notice of Proposed Rulemaking). Federal Register* 76, no. 143 (2011): 44512–31.

———. *Protecting Human Research Subjects: Status of Recommendations.* Washington, DC: U.S. Department of Health and Human Services, Office of Inspector General, 2000.

U.S. Department of Health and Human Services. Office of the Inspector General. *Institutional Review Boards: A Time for Reform.* Washington, DC: U.S. Department of Health and Human Services, 1998.

U.S. General Accounting Office. *Scientific Research: Continued Vigilance Critical to Protecting Human Subjects.* Washington, DC: U.S. General Accounting Office, 1996.

U.S. National Institutes of Health (NIH). "Protecting Human Research Participants (PHRP) Online Tutorial No Longer Available as of September 26, 2018." https://grants-nih-gov.proxy.bc.edu/grants/guide/notice-files/NOT-OD-18-221.html (accessed February 4, 2019).

Wagner, Todd H., Aman Bhandari, Gary L. Chadwick, and Daniel K. Nelson. "The Cost of Operating Institutional Review Boards (IRBs)." *Academic Medicine* 78, no. 6 (2003): 638–44.

Weber, Max. *Economy and Society: An Outline of Interpretive Sociology.* Translated by Guenther Roth and Claus Wittich. Berkeley: University of California Press, 1978.

West Virginia University. Human Research Protections Office. "Expedited Review Determination Checklist." https://oric.research.wvu.edu/files/d/591fa936-16f6-4292-828d-f0024ba76ff7/expedited-review-determination-checklist.pdf (accessed February 17, 2019).

White, Ronald F. "Institutional Review Board Mission Creep: The Common Rule, Social Science, and the Nanny State." *Independent Review* 11, no. 4 (2007): 547–64.

"Who Watches the Watchmen? Some Commercial Firms that Oversee the Ethics and Scrutiny of Clinical Trials Have Been Found Wanting; Human Volunteers in Research Deserve Better." *Nature* 476 (2011): 125.

Williams, Erin D. *Federal Protection for Human Research Subjects: An Analysis of the Common Rule and Its Interactions with FDA Regulations and the HIPAA Privacy Rule.* Washington, DC: Congressional Research Service, 2005.

Williams, Lauren. "Higher Ed Leaders Select the Most Effective Products of the Year." *University Business,* January 2014. https://universitybusiness.com/higher-ed-leaders-select-the-most-effective-products-of-the-year/.

WIRB-Copernicus Group. "2018 Single Review Service Fee Schedule." Princeton, NJ: WIRB-Copernicus.

Index

Lightning Source UK Ltd.
Milton Keynes UK
UKHW011447090622
404139UK00002B/151

9 781503 610149